Witness to a Conga

and other plays

prairie play SERIES

The Aberhart Summer
by Conni Massing
978-1-897126-40-5 | $13.95

At the Zenith of the Empire
by Stewart Lemoine
978-1-897126-15-8 | $18.95

Blood Relations and Other Plays
by Sharon Pollock
978-1-896300-64-1 | $19.95

Ethnicities
ed. Anne Nothof
978-1-896300-03-0 | $18.95

Harvest and Other Plays
by Ken Cameron
978-1-897126-67-7 | $19.95

The Hungry Spirit
by Elsie Park Gowan
978-0-920897-19-5 | $14.95

Martin Yesterday
by Brad Fraser
978-1-896300-26-9 | $13.95

Metastasis and Other Plays
by Gordon Pengilly
978-1-897126-40-0 | $19.95

The Minor Keys
by David Belke
978-1-896300-19-1 | $13.95

Naked At School
by Chris Craddock
978-1-896300-46-7 | $16.95

Nextfest Anthology
ed. Glenda Stirling
978-1-897126-04-2 | $18.95

Nextfest Anthology II
ed. Steve Pirot
978-1-897126-04-2 | $18.95

Poor Super Man
by Brad Fraser
978-0-920897-81-2 | $13.95

The Room with Five Walls
by Byrna Barclay
978-1-896300-78-8 | $16.95

Scraping the Surface
by Lyle Victor Albert
978-1-896300-33-7 | $12.95

Snake in Fridge
by Brad Fraser
978-1-896300-27-6 | $14.95

A Teatro Trilogy
by Stewart Lemoine
978-1-896300-80-1 | $18.95

The Ugly Man
by Brad Fraser
978-0-920897-43-0 | $13.95

The Wolf Plays
by Brad Fraser
978-0-920897-49-2 | $14.95

prairie play series no.29

Stewart Lemoine

Witness to a Conga and Other Plays

series editor: Diane Bessai

NeWest Press

Library and Archives Canada Cataloguing in Publication

Lemoine, Stewart, 1960–

Witness to a conga : and other plays / Stewart Lemoine.

Plays.

Contents: Happy toes — The oculist's holiday — Witness to a conga.

ISBN 978-1-897126-86-8

I. Title.

PS8573.E552W58 2011 C812'.54 C2011-901978-7

Editors: Diane Bessai & Anne Nothof

Cover and interior design: Natalie Olsen, Kisscut Design

Back cover photo: Briana Buckmaster

Author photo: Andrew MacDonald-Smith

Canada Council for the Arts / Conseil des Arts du Canada — Canadian Heritage / Patrimoine canadien — Alberta Foundation for the Arts — edmonton arts council

NeWest Press acknowledges the support of the Canada Council for the Arts, the Alberta Foundation for the Arts, and the Edmonton Arts Council for our publishing program. We acknowledge the financial support of the Government of Canada through the Canada Book Fund for our publishing activities.

#201, 8540 – 109 Street
Edmonton, Alberta T6G 1E6
780.432.9427
NeWest Press www.newestpress.com

No bison were harmed in the making of this book.

printed and bound in Canada 1 2 3 4 5 13 12 11 10

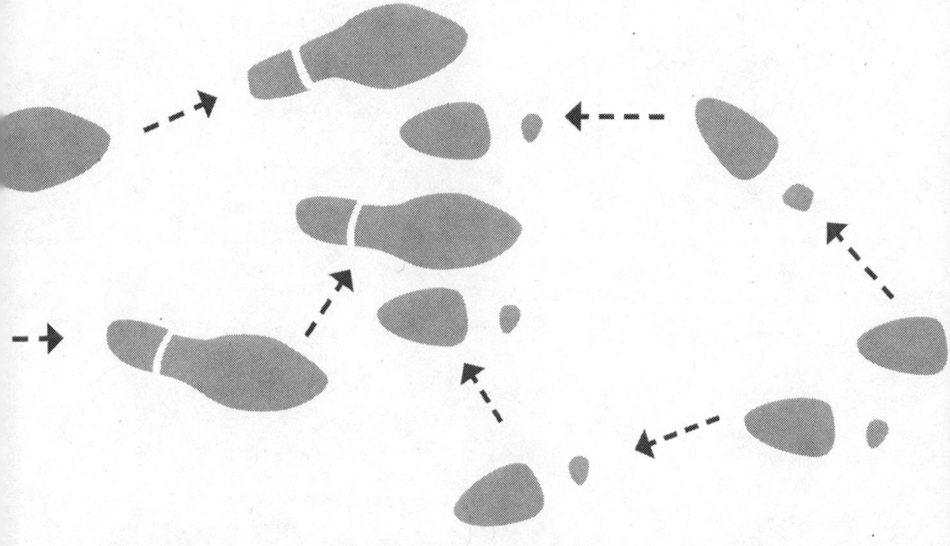

INTRODUCTION

Teatro La Quindicina first came into being at the inaugural Edmonton Fringe in 1982 and, with the exception of 1995, when we took a sabbatical, we presented productions at every edition of the Festival until 2002. In 2008, we returned to the Fringe, and the three plays collected in this volume represent the initial offerings in this second act of our relationship with Edmonton's unique theatrical institution. Our time away from the Festival was necessary and extremely productive in that it allowed us to strengthen our administrative structure, create a subscription series, and tour extensively. It was at the end of this five-year hiatus that I also stepped aside as the company's artistic director in order to devote myself more completely to writing.

When Jeff Haslam took the reins at Teatro, his first and most significant innovation was to change our programming from the standard fall-through-spring season to a more compressed spring/summer/early fall season which would include a Fringe presentation as part of the series. This has proven extremely popular with subscribers, and it's been a thrill to reconnect with the utterly intrepid and dauntlessly excited festival playgoers who descend on Old Strathcona every August.

The majority of Teatro's Fringe offerings in our first twenty years were new works, and in that time it was not uncommon for them also to feature extremely large casts. Plays like *The Swift Hotel* (17 actors), *My Miami Melody* (16), and the oft-revived *Cocktails at Pam's* (11) were veritable parties on the stage. Since part of our new mandate has been to present an annual big-cast riot-of-fun show show in July, my approach to what I write for the Festival has changed somewhat. The casts are smaller, though still fairly large by the standards of the Fringe, where the two-hander and the monodrama continue to prevail. The tone of the plays is somewhat different too, as we made a conscious decision to use this particular platform to present comedies of a more reflective sort.

Anyone reading or viewing *The Oculist's Holiday* is probably not going to be too surprised to learn that I've been reading a fair bit of F. Scott Fitzgerald lately, and while that particular play is a deliberate attempt to reinvent his narrative style in theatrical terms, I think his influence is felt in all three of these works. I think the unifying element here is that the characters in each play are all dealing with the adjusted expectations which one necessarily encounters when approaching mid-life. Fitzgerald's novels and short stories are very much concerned with this issue, it seems to me, so it's unfortunate that most people tend to read them when they're a bit too young to fully appreciate his insights. What I seem to have learned conclusively in the thirty years since I first read *The Great Gatsby* is that disappointments really are inevitable, and that some will consume us if we allow them to, but most can be transcended fairly easily if we apply ourselves with a little rigour.

All that said, thematic concerns are usually the last thing on my mind when I start to write a play. For me it's finding the incident which sets off a chain of events that'll come to constitute a story which, with luck, hasn't been told before. More often than not, these things come from my real life. A bank teller really did tell me she wished her branch would be hit by lightning. Passing through Lausanne on the train, I was so struck by the look of it that I was tempted to immediately disembark, despite not being my destination. (I didn't, though.) And finally, at an afternoon concert in Vienna's glittering Musikverein, I witnessed the extraordinary audience response when the Gothenburg Symphony Orchestra offered Arturo Márquez' *Conga del Fuego* as an encore after a program of Beethoven and Berlioz. As the heretofore prim and buttoned-down Viennese crowd erupted in a frenzy of whooping, stamping, and joyous hollering, I thought, "You really can't say no to a conga. Ever."

Stewart Lemoine
March, 2011

HAPPY TOES

(front to rear and left to right) Julien Arnold as Alex, Davina Stewart as Janine, Leona Brausen as Cora, Jeff Haslam as Tony, Ron Pederson as Edgar in *Happy Toes*. Photo by Dan Riedlhuber. Courtesy of the *Edmonton Journal.*

PRODUCTION HISTORY

Happy Toes was first performed by Teatro La Quindicina in August of 2008, at the Varscona Theatre in Edmonton. It was part of the Edmonton International Fringe Theatre Festival.

CAST

Tony – Jeff Haslam
Edgar – Ron Pederson
Alex – Julien Arnold
Cora – Leona Brausen
Janine – Davina Stewart

Director – Stewart Lemoine
Costume Designer – Leona Brausen
Lighting Designer – Bobby Smale
Set Designer – Jeff Haslam
Stage Manager – Rachel Rudd

CHARACTERS

Tony
Edgar
Alex
Cora
Janine

Tony, Alex, Cora, and Janine are all in their early to mid-forties. Edgar is in his early thirties.

SETTING

Happy Toes takes place in an unnamed Canadian city in the present day: The action spans the spring and fall of a single year.

In the premiere production, the coffee shop and bank counter were fixed settings on either side of the stage. All other scenes took place in a central carpeted area with four moveable chairs. Since the Varscona stage is necessarily a black box during the Fringe, all set pieces and furnishings were light-coloured wood, which helped establish a bright and airy visual tone.

MUSIC

The music which played at the beginning and end of the play, and in transitional scenes was *Les Barricades Mystérieuses,* a piece originally written for solo harpsichord by François Couperin (1668–1733). Though we began and ended with the harpsichord version, the excerpts heard over the course included solo arrangements for piano, lute, banjo, and harp, and in the concert scene, Alex and Cora listened to a chamber arrangement for woodwinds and strings by Thomas Adès, which features a prominent clarinet part for Edgar. The appeal of Couperin's piece, with regard to *Happy Toes*, lies in the way it maintains an unerring, almost methodical sense of forward motion, even in the face of some fairly unexpected harmonic shifts and suspensions.

HAPPY TOES

Scene One

Edgar and Tony enter as music plays and sit in chairs. There's a little table between them and they have cups of coffee. Music fades.

Edgar: The strangest thing happened today. I was doing some banking . . .

Tony: Oh yes?

Edgar: Yes, I was just depositing some cheques from my students, and it had been raining, so the teller asked whether it looked like it was going to clear anytime soon. I said it didn't seem likely and then she said that she wished it was still thundering out because that meant there was a better chance the bank would be hit by lightning.

Tony: Really? That is a bit strange. Must have shaken your confidence a little, as you handed over your money. I mean, to have the custodian of your funds wishing the place would maybe burn.

Edgar: It was less dramatic than that. She just said that if it happened, there'd probably be a long blackout and she'd get to go home early.

Tony: That's a bit better, I guess . . . But she's lucky you weren't a bank inspector. What did you say?

Edgar: I said that the bank would get hit if that's what it deserved. She laughed a little. Politely, I'd guess.

Tony: Do you think a bank can deserve to be struck by lightning?

Edgar: Well, not the structure necessarily, but maybe the people who run it. No, you know, I'll just say that I don't think anyone deserves to be struck by lightning.

Tony: So your remark to the teller was . . .

Edgar: Pointless. A spit in the wind.

Tony: You could have just bawled her out for wishing an inconvenience on all the customers who were planning to bank later in the day.

Edgar: I thought about it. But you know . . .

Tony: Yes?

Edgar: When she said it . . . when she wished the bank would be struck so that she might be free . . . she was radiant. She wasn't irritated at all, just sort of briefly elated by possibility. Why would I want to squelch that, particularly?

Tony: There's no earthly reason to do so.

Edgar: Yet certain people *would* do it. You even thought of a couple of valid objections.

Tony: Yes, but like you, I probably wouldn't have given voice to them. Objections can and should be part of an overall contemplation of life, but there's surprisingly little to be gained from sharing them at every available opportunity.

Edgar: Does the same go for praise, then?

Tony: One can overdo that. Look, here's Alex.

Alex enters.

Edgar: Aha, yes. Good morning, Alex.

Alex: Edgar. Tony. Hello.

Tony: Good morning.

Edgar: We don't see you running anymore.

Alex: No, well, I guess I've stopped for a while. I shouldn't have.

Tony: It's okay. You can stop and start. It's not bad for you.

Edgar: Yes, we're just glad you're not running with other people. You know, cheating.

Alex: Cheating. Right. With a bitter little laugh. That.

Edgar: Alex?

Alex looks from one to the other.

Alex: I . . .

Tony: Something is troubling you. Can we help?

Alex: I think my wife is having an affair.

Tony: Oh no.

Edgar: That's terrible. You're certain?

Alex: I think so. It's very peculiar. Can I tell you a couple of things?

Edgar: Of course. Or maybe . . . To Tony. I'm presuming, perhaps. You might not want to know . . .

Tony: I offered to help. If listening is helpful, we should do that.

Alex: Thank you. It's been going on for nearly two weeks. I come home and she has beautiful dinners prepared and we eat by candlelight and there's wine and she speaks in the most intimate way and initiates the most surprising . . .

Well, I don't think I need to explain all that in detail. But then she meets me for lunch and she's made reservations in restaurants where we sit in dim little corners, and yesterday she said she had a surprise for me if I'd book a couple of hours in the early afternoon, so I did and she picked me up and we drove to a hotel. Near the airport. And we checked in.

Edgar: And then?

Alex: Do I really have to say?

Edgar: Well, I'm not following entirely. It doesn't exactly sound like cheating behaviour on her part.

Tony: Unless what you're saying is that your wife is having an affair . . . and it's with you.

Alex: Yes. Exactly. That's what I think is happening.

Edgar: I'm not sure that's a very valid cause for worry.

Alex: Isn't it? Why would she be doing this all of a sudden? Something must have gone wrong. I mean . . . I thought our marriage was great. It's been fine for twelve years and out of the blue there's this and it's just so drastic and strange and I feel like I must have been missing something that should have been obvious to me, and I'm so afraid of what it might turn out to be.

Edgar: You haven't asked her? In your intimate talks?

Alex: Oh no. It's . . . not that kind of intimacy.

Edgar: Oh. Wow.

Alex: Yes, she's sort of an unstoppable train.

Tony: So it isn't completely unpleasant?

Alex: In the moment, no. But afterward . . . the guilt just devours me. I'm nervous at work. I'm afraid to go home . . . Listen, I'm sorry. You must think this is ridiculous and I'm sorry to burden you with it. I just thought maybe if I said all this out loud it'd seem preposterous and I could dismiss it, but I don't think that's the case.

Tony: Well, there's no need to apologize. You've given us something to think about, certainly.

Edgar: Yes, it's a remarkable quandary and I don't think I've got much to offer in the way of advice.

Alex: Oh, that's fine. You offered to help and then did just that by letting me speak. I should be off anyway. Wouldn't you know, I'm meeting her for lunch.

Edgar: Oh. Well . . . Squeezing his hands. Courage.

Tony: Give her our regards.

Alex: I'll do my best to work that in, but . . . You know, two weeks ago I'd have said I was completely happy. Pause. Well, good-bye.

Tony: Good-bye.

Edgar: Bye-bye.

Alex exits.

Edgar: Well well . . . what a thing.

Tony: Isn't it.

Edgar: Poor Alex. Just completely happy and then . . . I wonder if *I'll* ever be completely happy.

Tony: I don't know. I don't know if that's possible. For anyone, I mean. Not just you.

Edgar: Why?

Tony: Well . . . completely happy . . . What does that actually mean? Shouldn't it mean happy for good? Permanently?

Edgar: No, I think it'd be more a matter of being as happy as one could possibly be in a particular instance.

Tony: Happy from your head right down to your toes?

Edgar: Exactly.

A pause. They consider.

Tony: So, here's a question for your bank teller . . .

Edgar: Yes?

Tony: What's at home?

Edgar: What?

Tony: Didn't she say that if the bank were struck by lightning, she'd get to go home? She didn't say she'd get off work or leave early, did she?

Edgar: No, you're right. Is that odd?

Tony: Well, when people get unexpected time off, don't they usually try to maximize it with some sort of fun excursion? Lunch, a movie, shopping . . .

Edgar: Yeah, and she just wanted to go home.

Tony: She must just love it there.

Edgar: Or else she's got a bunch of chores she needs to catch up on.

Tony: But you said she was radiant at the prospect of –

Edgar: Of going home! Yes, she was. You're right to have commented on this.

Tony: What sort of person was she? Young?

Edgar: Not especially. She seemed like more of a supervisor teller type. Cora . . . that's her name.

Tony: Is it odd then that she'd be so frank with a customer? That's more what you'd expect from a junior teller, wouldn't you say?

Edgar: From a coltish trainee? You're probably right. So this is seeming pretty unusual.

Tony: I think it is. She's maybe a little reckless.

Edgar: Yet still a homebody.

Tony: A figure of real fascination.

Edgar: Yes, like Alex's wife.

Tony: Right. Her. What's her name? Janice? Justine? Janine.

Edgar: Janine! The reason Alex has a fear of going home. But Cora at the bank has no such fear.

Tony: Yet she can't be at home when she most wishes to be.

Edgar: Barring natural disaster. Shaking his head. These are troubled people.

Tony: Troubled? Or troubling?

Edgar: What's the difference? Things are out of whack in both cases. I'm going back to the bank.

Tony: Why?

Edgar: If you'd seen her . . . I just really want an answer because I think there's a fairly good chance it'll be delightful.

Tony: So, enjoying contemplation of the vast array of possibilities isn't really a viable option for you?

Edgar: No. That sort of thing is for . . . well, for you, I guess. Hey, do you want a ticket to my concert tonight? It's our little chamber group . . . in the church hall. Taking out tickets. I've got some free tickets. I mean they're free at the door too, but here's one now!

Tony: Oh, thanks.

Edgar: You don't have to use it.

Tony: No, I expect I will. I enjoy those events. I get to think a lot during them. That's permitted, right?

Edgar: It's what they're for. Do you want two tickets? You can have –

Tony: No, that's fine. One's good. I'll see you after, maybe?

Edgar: Yes, and who knows what I'll have to share?

Tony: Good luck. I hope you don't get slapped.

Edgar: It's all about risk.

Tony: Meh.

They exit in opposite directions.

Scene Two

Cora is at a counter. Edgar approaches her.

Cora: Oh hello. You're back.

Edgar: You remember me?

Cora: Sure. Well . . . not your name.

Edgar: Edgar.

Cora: Yes. That was it. Did I make a mistake? I didn't give you a balance. I'm sorry if –

Edgar: No, it's something else. I wanted to ask you about a different thing. Cora.

Cora: Oh. Alright. You have some questions about your account?

Edgar: No no. It was . . . Well, you remember I was here during that storm this morning and you said you hoped the bank would get hit by lightning so you could go home early?

Cora: Oh yes, I'm sorry about that. It wasn't really appropriate of me. It's a huge inconvenience for everyone when the bank closes down.

Edgar: Well sure, but that's not what I want to talk about. You really don't have to apologize.

Cora: Alright.

Edgar: In fact you might recall that I suggested people here might deserve to be struck and electrocuted, and that's gotta be fairly inappropriate too.

Cora: Maybe, but at least it's funny.

Edgar: Okay, well, that's a relief, but –

Cora: Yes? This is going somewhere, right? You have a question?

Edgar: Cora, what's at home? Why would you specifically want to be there during your found time? You know, instead of out and about?

Cora: After a pause. Umm . . . Well . . .

Edgar: You know I've just realized how truly odd this question must seem, coming from a random customer, so if you don't care to answer, by all means –

Cora: No no, it's okay. I don't know why you'd come in just to ask that and nothing else, but . . . you get a bee in your bonnet and . . . I think all it is is that at home I'm at my most relaxed.

Edgar: And here you're tense?

Cora: Not tense. Just attentive, necessarily. All day.

Edgar: Oh. Pause. Good answer there, Cora.

Cora: Thanks.

Edgar: I don't know why it wasn't more obvious to me.

Cora: Maybe you aren't really relaxed at home. Some people just aren't, I think.

Edgar: Yes, well, your home becomes something a bit different when you start to give clarinet lessons there. Which is what I do.

Cora: Oh, that's interesting.

Edgar: That's what all those cheques are for. That I deposit. They're from my students. From their parents, actually.

Cora: You teach clarinet. You're a music teacher?

Edgar: Well, I play also. In ensembles and sometimes with the orchestra.

Cora: That's interesting. I always wanted to learn an instrument. I don't know anything about the clarinet, but . . . Looking off. Oh, now people are waiting. We shouldn't really be chatting.

Edgar: Oh, right. Sorry. Looking off. Sorry, sir. I'll be gone in a second. To Cora. I know exactly how much he hates me. I'll see you next time, I guess, and thanks again for your forbearance.

Cora: Not a problem. Have a nice day.

Edgar: Bye-bye.

He exits. Cora signals to the next customer. The light fades on her.

Scene Three

Tony is sitting on a bench, outdoors. Alex walks by, a little preoccupied.

Tony: Alex!

Alex: Oh hi. Tony! Again!

Tony: I'd ask how lunch was, but that now seems like an outrageously personal question.

Alex: It was kind of what I expected. Sitting. We went to a restaurant, but first we spent some time in the car.

Tony: Driving?

Alex: No. Just . . . in the parkade. I'm glad we have those tinted windows. I don't know that they're entirely legal, but then neither is . . .

He lowers his head and covers his face with his hands.

Tony: So you didn't talk about . . . things? Afterward.

Alex: No. In the restaurant, it was just . . . renovations she'd like us to do. The neighbour's holiday . . .

Tony: So . . . as though nothing else had happened?

Alex: That's always how it is. It's like there are two completely disconnected women, and if I were to speak frankly to either of them, I think they'd be shattered. She would. No, they. Ahhh . . .

Tony: It's an unpleasant prospect, but confrontation might actually lead you to a happy resolution.

Alex: You think?

Tony: I've thought about your options. I don't know that there are any.

Alex: I thought about hiring a private detective. Isn't that what cuckolds usually do?

Tony: Sure, but it's kind of an inappropriate step for a lover to take. And like it or not –

Alex: Yes, I see what you're saying. Well I think I'm just going to stay the course with avoidance for now.

Tony: Sure. There's lots of precedent for that. Clouds shift. Winds change.

Alex: I told her I had to work late tonight. I don't, but I'm just not ready to go another round.

Tony: You know that's not avoidance, right?

Alex: What?

Tony: It's active deception.

Alex: Oh dear God, you're right. Still –

Tony: It's okay. You're entitled to have time alone if you think you need it.

Alex: I don't actually have anything to do at work. It'll be awful. I'll just sit there, feeling guilty. Maybe I should go to a movie.

Tony: You know, Edgar is playing in a concert tonight. You could go to that.

Alex: Yeah? What is it exactly?

Tony: Chamber music. I'm not sure what all is on the programme.

Alex: But it might be pleasant? Soothing?

Tony: It's a really great forum for private thinking.

Alex: Oh, I don't know if I'm up for that.

Tony: Then just pay attention.

Alex: Are you going?

Tony: Probably. But . . . Taking out ticket. I'm going to give you this ticket. I can get another one at the door. I might be a little late anyway.

Alex: What'll I owe you?

Tony: Oh nothing. They're free.

Alex: Really? So are they not very good chamber musicians?

Tony: No, I think they're excellent. They just have their own . . . code of conduct. And expectations.

Alex: Okay, great. I'm glad I ran into you, Tony. This has been helpful. I know it's still just avoidance but –

Tony: But now with a dash of cultural enrichment.

Alex: A soundtrack makes everything better.

Tony: Yup.

Scene Four

Edgar is in the coffee shop, reading a magazine. Cora enters.

Cora: Oh, hello again. Edgar.

Edgar: Cora! You're homeward bound finally?

Cora: Oh no. It'll be a couple of hours yet. This is just my coffee break. I'm glad to see you, though. I'm sorry our conversation was interrupted.

Edgar: Well, I suppose it couldn't be helped.

Cora: If that fellow behind you had taken the time to make sure his twenties were all face up with the heads on the same side before coming in, then we might have had an extra minute or two.

Edgar: I knew he was trouble. So did you have a question for me maybe? Something musical?

Cora: Well, yes. You said you give clarinet lessons and that made me wonder about music lessons in general. Do you think it's really possible for someone my age to take up an instrument?

Edgar: It's not impossible.

Cora: But . . .

Edgar: But it doesn't often work. Statistically. I'm sorry.

Cora: No no, don't be sorry. I've heard that sort of thing before and it's your field, so I certainly believe you.

Edgar: It's not just *your* age. It's mine too. I mean, if I hadn't started when I was nine . . . Sometimes adults have more luck with the guitar or the piano.

Cora: Why do you think that is?

Edgar: I guess it's because one finger is one note on those instruments. Maybe . . .

Cora: That makes sense. So if I'm good on an adding machine . . .

Edgar: You still might not be ready for chording. I'm sorry. I don't mean to be discouraging. You should try whatever you want. There are no rules.

Cora: Well, you know, I think maybe what I want is to be a more educated listener.

Edgar: Oh, for sure. Hearing it well can be as satisfying as doing it. And we who make the music are always happy to enlarge the audience. So, to that end . . .

Cora: Yes?

Edgar: *Taking out a ticket.* I'm playing in a concert tonight. It's chamber music, but really pleasant. Accessible. If you want to come, I've got some free tickets.

Cora: Really? Just like that? I get to hear you play?

Edgar: If you're not doing anything. It's at 7:30. *Handing her a ticket.* The address is on here.

Cora: Oh yes, I know where that is. But I can certainly pay.

Edgar: Actually, it's free for everyone, but we find if we give out tickets, people are more likely to show up.

Cora: Smart. Well, I'll definitely be there.

Edgar: Good. Stick around after. Someone usually brings cheese.

Cora: Nice! Well I should go, but I'll see you later.

Edgar: Did you want to bring a friend? I have more tickets.

Cora: No, that's fine. It'll just be me. See ya.

Edgar: Bye-bye.

She exits. He sits alone for a moment. Janine enters and notices him.

Janine: Oh . . . hello! Um . . .

Edgar: Hi! Janine! It's . . . Edgar.

Janine: Yes, that's right. Edgar. Alex's friend . . . from that running group . . . that he was in . . . when he ran.

Edgar: I just saw Alex this morning, actually. He said you were having lunch together today.

Janine: Oh really? He did?

Edgar: I think. Or maybe he meant . . . uh . . .

Janine: Oh I'm just teasing. Yes, we just had lunch. It was highly satisfactory. Better than running, probably. Do you still do that?

Edgar: Oh yeah.

Janine: Right, you play the . . . oboe?

Edgar: The clarinet.

Janine: Right. Edgar the clarinetist. And you run because it's all about your lungs. You see, I remember. How's your other friend? The zillionaire.

Edgar: Tony? I'm not sure he's worth that yet. I have a connection at the bank, though. I could probably check.

Janine: What was his money from? Peat? Sod?

Edgar: Dirt. It was a family dirt business. His dad invented a particularly good kind, and they never looked back.

Janine: How do you invent dirt? It wouldn't occur to me to try doing that.

Edgar: I know what you mean. There are just so many good ideas in the world and I'm not having anywhere near enough of them. Tony's fine, by the way. Idle. Rich.

Janine: And happy?

Edgar: He stays on a pretty even keel. Unlike most people, I think.

Janine: Right. You see, I'm still struggling toward that. I'm going for a manicure, but first I need a coffee. It's an endless struggle. Always uphill.

Edgar: You don't ask to be born. Don't they give you coffee in salons? As part of the pampering?

Janine: Oh, but it's terrible. And it's always in clear glass mugs, which I just can't bear.

Edgar: Is there a special occasion looming? Something you're primping for? Someone?

Janine: Edgar! What are you suggesting?

Edgar: Uh . . . nothing? I'm sorry.

Janine: Oh, I'm just teasing you again. Lighten up. Actually I'll be spending an evening at home alone. Alex is working late tonight and I suppose it was inevitable that might happen when I insist on meeting him for lunch as often as I do.

Edgar: Well, if you're bored and lonely, you can always come to a concert I'm playing in tonight. It's a chamber music thing. I've got free tickets . . . Taking them out. Maybe you want one?

Janine: Oh . . . That might be interesting. I never go to chamber music. I don't know anyone who does. Is it formal?

Edgar: Not at all. But you won't be shunned for having nice nails.

Janine: Fine then. I'll probably come. But I'm happy to pay for the ticket.

Edgar: Oh no, they're all free. No one's paying.

Janine: Then why are you doing it?

Edgar: Uhh . . .

Janine: Never mind. I'm sure it'll be clear.

Edgar: You can have two tickets. If you want to bring a friend.

Janine: Oh, I never do that. See you later.

She exits. Light fades.

Scene Five

A row of four chairs. Cora is sitting in one on the end, looking at a leaflet. Alex enters, also with a leaflet. He looks at the chairs.

Alex: No one's sitting here?

Cora: I don't think so.

Alex: Oh. Good.

He sits, one seat away from Cora. They look at their leaflets.

Alex: Actually, do you mind . . .

He moves into the seat next to hers.

It kind of drives me crazy at things when single people leave gaps. Then couples and friends can't sit together.

Cora: Yeah, I know what you mean. It's fine, though . . . Looking around. It seems like it won't be that full.

Alex: Maybe not. I'm new to this sort of thing.

Cora: Oh, me too. A friend gave me a free ticket.

Alex: I think that's something we all have in common.

Cora: I know one of the musicians a little. Hardly at all. The clarinetist.

Alex: Oh yeah? Edgar?

Cora: Yes. You know him too?

Alex: I do. He didn't give me the ticket, but . . . well I guess indirectly he did. I'm Alex.

Cora: Alex, I'm Cora.

Alex: Shaking her hand. Nice to meet you, Cora.

They look at their leaflets.

So what are we in for?

Cora: I don't know. None of these things listed really mean much to me, but that's probably my fault.

Alex: I don't know. Looks deliberately obscure to me.

Cora: I guess it's an adventure either way.

Alex: So how is it you know Edgar?

Cora: From the bank. Where he banks. I'm a teller.

Alex: Oh.

Cora: And you?

Alex: I'm a lawyer. With an insurance company. But you were actually asking how I know Edgar.

Cora: Yes.

Alex: From running. We ran together. In a group.

Cora: But then you dispersed?

Alex: I just stopped. Running.

Cora: Was it hard on you? I'd think it might be after a while.

Alex: A bit of that, and it can be boring. I'll probably do it again. I'm kind of in the mood to be bored.

Cora: Well maybe you're in luck. I think they're about to start.

Alex: Oh yes. Well here's hoping for . . . something.

Music is heard. They listen and the light fades.

Scene Six

After a moment light is restored and Alex and Cora are seen applauding politely at the conclusion of the piece.

Alex: Well that was . . . gentle.

Cora: It was. It made me happy.

Alex: Me too. I didn't always pay attention.

Cora: I did. I think I did. Not in the way I do when I'm counting money, or . . . It's just very satisfying.

Alex: It is, but I wonder if it'll get a little more vigourous. I might need caffeine before long.

Cora: There's free coffee, just in that other room. I saw it as I came in. There's an urn.

Alex: Oh? Maybe I'll . . . Is this an intermission? It seems a little soon for that.

Cora: Looking at leaflet. It's just a pause. It says they'll take a few minutes between the pieces to rearrange the music stands.

Alex: Oh, great. I'm going to get a coffee. Do you want one?

Cora: Sure, why not. I don't want to fade after such a promising start.

Alex: Getting up. Exactly. Cream and sugar?

Cora: Yes please.

Alex: Be right back.

He exits. Cora sits and peruses her leaflet. After a moment Janine enters. She approaches the row of chairs.

Janine: Excuse me, are any of these free?

Cora: *Indicating.* Someone's using this one, but these other two are available.

Janine: Oh, good. *Sitting in the aisle seat.* I was a little late, so I had to go to the balcony. It's kind of steep, though. I didn't feel safe.

Cora: Well, you were right to move down, then.

Janine: I thought so. I don't think these are meant to be white-knuckle events.

Cora: Probably not.

Janine: *Looking at her leaflet.* Oh say, all my favourites.

Cora: Really?

Janine: Mm . . . no. It's my first time.

Cora: Mine too. It's pleasant so far, though.

Janine: And you can't beat the price.

Cora: Do you know any of the musicians?

Janine: One, a little. He's a friend of my husband's. From his running group.

Cora: Oh, that's funny because . . . Well, maybe it's not. It's probably a big group, so it'd make sense that . . .

Janine: I beg your pardon?

Cora: Sorry, I'm just babbling. Thinking out loud.

Janine: Oh, then I shouldn't listen.

They laugh. Alex enters with two cups of coffee.

Alex: Here we are. Excuse me . . . wha . . .

Janine: Alex?

Alex: Janine. Hi.

Janine: You're here. You're here?

Alex: Yes. You're here too . . .

Janine: You're not at work?

Alex: No. I . . . came here instead.

Janine: Evidently.

Alex: I got a free ticket.

Janine: Yes, well . . . who didn't? Why do you have two coffees?

Alex: Oh . . . this is . . . Handing a cup to Cora . . . yours.

Janine: What . . . who . . .

Alex: Cora, this is my wife, Janine.

Cora: Oh, hello. I mean, not . . . hello exactly. We've already been speaking.

Janine: Alex, what's going on? You said you had to work late tonight and instead you're at a concert. With a woman I don't know and have never heard of.

Alex: Janine, hang on. What are you implying? That's so ridiculous.

Janine: Ridiculous? Is that what it is when you lie to your wife about your plans for the evening?

Alex: It's not . . . I just didn't . . . I don't want to get into this here.

Janine: Get into *this?* So you'll admit it's *something?* We have an issue?

Alex: No . . . I . . .

Janine: I think you're having an affair. Maybe it's just starting, or maybe it's been going on for years, but it's what I think, based on what I see and so –

Alex: Whoa now, Janine! I'm gonna stop you right there. I haven't said anything, but for the past two weeks, I think *you've* been the one having an affair. All the unexpected trysts and mad passionate love-making out of the blue, provoked by God knows what because you won't talk to me about it or let me get a word in before you turn into a tornado followed by a tidal wave. It was exciting in its way, but I don't know what you're doing, Janine. You're acting like a woman in the midst of the most torrid love affair anyone ever imagined, but I don't know what it's got to do with me. You're cheating on me, and you're cheating with me, and you're cheating me, and just plain cheating me and cheating me, and I don't understand, and so I didn't want to go home for more of that tonight, so I came here and I sat next to this lady and she's really very nice, but now I wish I hadn't met her because we've probably wrecked her night.

Janine has sat with her mouth open, for most of this.

Janine: Oh . . . no . . .

She starts to cry. A little at first, then abruptly she gives way and just shakes and sobs and sputters uncontrollably. Alex and Cora look around, a little concerned.

Alex: Touching Janine's shoulder gently. Janine, please . . . Maybe we should . . .

Janine: Still weeping, recoiling and pushing him away at the same time. No . . . no . . . go away. I can't . . . see you . . .

Cora: Getting up. I should excuse myself. I don't think this is any of my –

Janine: No . . . you . . . stay . . .

She grabs her arm and pulls her back. Cora sits in the seat next to Janine.

I'm sorry . . . Please . . .

Cora: Oh . . .

She tentatively embraces the sobbing Janine.

I'll stay. It's alright. But let's be quiet so they can start the music.

Janine nods and attempts to cry in a more restrained manner. Alex looks at Cora perplexedly. She gestures for him to go. He shrugs and exits after a moment. The lights fade on Cora gently rocking Janine and patting her.

Scene Seven

Alex is standing, looking a little dazed. Edgar enters.

Edgar: Alex? *You're* here?

Alex: Yes. Shouldn't you be –

Edgar: The next piece is just piano and strings. I'm not in it. There was a little commotion, apparently. Do you know what –

Alex: Yes, it was Janine, unfortunately. She's still in there. Crying.

Edgar: What? Did you come together? She said you were working.

Alex: Yes. That's what I told her.

Edgar: Oh no. And then I gave her a ticket. I'm so sorry. Wait, no . . . I didn't know you were going to be here.

Alex: Tony gave me his ticket.

Edgar: So he's not here?

Alex: I haven't seen him. He said he was coming anyway, but he'd probably be late. Are you mad?

Edgar: No, I'm just confused. Why is Janine crying?

Alex: We sort of got into it over the whole infidelity thing. I accused her of cheating on me and she just lost it.

Edgar: I guess that's not too surprising. I mean, guilty or not, it's still gotta –

Alex: She accused me first. She said I was cheating with the woman who was sitting next to me. And I wasn't. I've been completely faithful and all I did was lie about what I was doing tonight.

Edgar: And the other woman implicated in this? A total stranger?

Alex: To me, certainly. She knows you. From the bank.

Edgar: Cora?

Alex: Yes. Nice lady. We chatted a bit.

Edgar: Where is she now?

Alex: She's still inside. She's taking care of Janine.

Edgar: I . . . uh . . .

Alex: What?

Edgar: I don't know. I'm right out of questions. No, here's one. What are you going to do?

Alex: I don't know. I think all I can do is wait till she calms down.

Edgar: That's probably not going to happen while they're playing Scriabin in there.

Tony enters.

Tony: Oh, hey fellas. Sorry I'm late. To Edgar. Why aren't you onstage?

Edgar: It's kind of involved. Wait, no it isn't. I'm not in this piece. But something else is going on. Alex here is in trouble.

Tony: Oh?

Alex: Yes. It's Janine. She's in there and –

Tony: Why? Did she follow you here?

Edgar: I gave her a ticket.

Tony: Oh-oh. So . . .

Alex: She's upset.

Edgar: She's crying. A lot.

Alex: I shouldn't have said what I did. But she – . . . oh.

Cora approaches.

Cora: Excuse me, Alex . . . Oh, hi Edgar. I noticed you weren't playing. Is it because –

Edgar: No, it's fine. I don't have a part in that piece. I sure do here though.

Cora: Alex, I just came to say . . . I'm taking your wife home.

Alex: Oh . . . you're sure? I suppose that's . . . best. If it's what she wants. I guess I'll see her there later.

Cora: No, I meant . . . I'm taking her to my home.

Alex: Oh?

Cora: Yes. It's no trouble, really. She just needs to be away from . . .

Alex: Me?

Cora: Well . . . yes . . .

Alex: Alright. So . . . I guess . . . call if anything happens I should know about. Giving her a business card. These are my numbers.

Cora: Thanks. Edgar, sorry I can't hear the rest. I liked that first piece quite a lot.

Edgar: Oh. Good. I . . . hope you can come again sometime.

Cora: So do I. Now good-night. To Tony. I didn't meet you. I'm Cora.

Tony: Oh. Tony.

She nods and exits quickly.

Edgar: To Alex. So . . . what do you want to do?

Alex: I don't know. I think I'm going to go splash water on my face. And then . . . No, that's all I know.

He exits.

Edgar: I'll bet you have some questions.

Tony: Just one. Who's Cora?

Edgar: She's the teller from my bank.

Tony: From this morning? The one who wanted to get hit by lightning?

Edgar: Yup.

Tony: I guess she kinda got her wish.

Edgar: Yes, and now I feel terrible, which you'll remember was not my intent. I'm going backstage now. I can't let my reed dry out.

Tony: I'll see you after. We'll discuss the music, of course.

Edgar: Right. Music might be in tough, what with a marital breakdown and eight kinds of cheese. Hey, why were you late?

Tony: Are you mad?

Edgar: No, it's just . . . you don't work. Why would you be late for anything?

Tony: My car was being serviced. I had to pick it up.

Edgar: Oh. I guess not everything's interesting and dramatic.

Tony: Fortunately.

Edgar exits. Tony looks at his ticket, then starts to exit. Alex returns.

Tony: Alex, you're –

Alex: Not looking better in the least. I can't find a bathroom. I'm leaving.

Tony: That's understandable. I'm sorry about all this.

Alex: Oh, don't be. It's not your fault.

Tony: Well, technically, you're here at my suggestion.

Alex: Right, and hey, what do you know . . . I'm not afraid to go home. *Glumly.* That's progress, right?

Tony: Sure, I guess you can spin it that way. So . . . what do you think –

Alex: *Holding up a hand.* Nothing. I can't . . . think . . . anything. Good night.

Tony: Good night.

They exit in opposite directions as lights fade.

Scene Eight

At the bank. Edgar approaches Cora's wicket.

Cora: Oh, Edgar. Hi.

Edgar: Hi Cora. I don't actually have any banking to do. *Taking out a bank card.* But I could make a withdrawal if that would buy us a little time to talk.

Cora: Well, we'll see. It's not so busy just at the moment.

Edgar: I really just wanted to apologize again for what I put you through the other night.

Cora: Oh, it's fine. I was sorry to have missed the rest of the concert, but I expect there'll be others.

Edgar: Well, I was thinking more about the huge imposition that got heaved your way. You forced to care for a strange lady.

Cora: It wasn't that much trouble. I took her home, put her in the guest room, and didn't see her again till I got home from work yesterday.

Edgar: So she's still there? At your house?

Cora: Till the weekend. Then she's leaving town for a bit. Tonight, I'm taking her to her house to collect some clothes.

Edgar: Will Alex be there?

Cora: I talked to him. He's agreed to be out.

Edgar: So they're not –

Cora: No, not yet. I don't . . . I shouldn't say this, because they're your friends really, but I don't see much hope for them.

Edgar: That's so strange. What do you think went wrong?

Cora: I don't know. She asked if it was alright for her not to explain anything and I said I was just fine with that, because I really really am.

Edgar: She must have other actual friends that she could be staying with.

Cora: I think that goes back to her not wanting to explain things.

Edgar: Right, well . . . you're sure you're fine with it? There's nothing I can do to help?

Cora: No. I don't think so.

Edgar: I am struck by a certain irony, and that is that you said home was where you didn't have to be attentive. Now it seems you do, and I continue to blame myself for this.

Cora: Well stop that. Janine's just fine to have in the house. She vacuumed parts of it I didn't even know existed.

Edgar: And maybe it's nice for you to have someone else there for a change.

Cora: I don't know what you mean by that. I have two teenaged sons. Big ones too.

Edgar: Oh . . . I never thought . . . I just didn't . . .

Cora: You thought I lived a quiet life alone? With only my gentle self in . . . what . . . a cottage? With a rose garden? *Laughing uproariously.* I'm sorry, that's just too funny. I don't have a husband anymore, if you're wondering about that, but rest assured, I consider it among my many blessings. Oh, and people are lining up now. Will there be anything else today?

Edgar: I don't think there will. Thanks, Cora. You've given me lots to think about.

Cora: Great. Let me know about your next concert.

Edgar: Will do. Bye-bye.

He exits. Cora laughs again, then calls off.

Cora: I can help you down here, sir.

Scene Nine

Alex sits at a table in the coffee shop. He has a cup of coffee and a large envelope sits on the table in front of him. Tony enters.

Tony: Alex, hi.

Alex: Hi, Tony. Thanks for coming.

Tony: Sure, maybe I'll just get a –

Alex: Edgar's already here. I think he's getting yours.

Tony: *Looking off.* Oh, yes, you're right.

Alex: Please sit.

Tony: Thanks. How've you been?

Alex raises an eyebrow.

Sorry, I guess that's a loaded question.

Alex: Yeah, it's funny. How've I been? Pause. I don't actually know.

Edgar enters with two cups of coffee.

Edgar: Hi there. Setting a cup in front of Tony. Here ya go.

Tony: Thanks.

Edgar: Sitting. It's nice to see you Alex. We've certainly been thinking about you.

Tony: Yes, and I was glad you called.

Edgar: I should have called. It's just difficult to know what's . . . uh –

Alex: Appropriate? Expected? Really, it's fine. We're friends, but we're not terribly close. We haven't been, and yet . . . now . . .

Tony: You need to talk to someone?

Edgar: That's fine. We're here.

Alex: Listen, it's been over a week. Things have changed . . . irrevocably. Janine and that woman Cora, who's a friend of yours and also just very kind and gracious by the way . . . They came and collected her things. Her clothes, mostly, but all of them, you see? I had thought maybe some basics, enough for a week or two away, but she took everything that was hers in the house. Not the china or kitchen things or anything like that, just her personal stuff. All of it. Gone.

Edgar: Aw, Alex, that's . . .

Alex: Yup. And there was a note. *Taking a note from a pocket.* Do you want to hear what she said?

Tony: We don't have to, unless, you –

Alex: No, I don't mind. You already knew a little of what was going on, so this may clarify things. *Handing it to Edgar.* I won't read it though.

Edgar: *Reading.* "Alex, I'm so sorry for doing what I did. I've misused the most basic gestures of devotion and affection and know there can be no hope for us. All further contact we have will have to be through lawyers."

Tony: And that's it?

Alex: Yup.

Edgar: This is terrible. You must have so many questions.

Alex: I do. But I don't think the answers are going to be much comfort. There's one thing, though, I need to talk to you about.

Tony: Of course.

Edgar: Please, whatever it is, go ahead.

Alex: I just want to know everything you know about my wife. Can you tell me what you remember about her?

Edgar: I . . . think I only met her twice. The other day when I gave her that ticket, and before that when we all met after that charity run thing we were all in. That's when you met her too, Tony, right?

Tony: Yes. That was it. It was last summer, so not quite a year ago. I do remember it, though, because I've been thinking about it a little. In the light of what's happened.

Alex: I . . . could say something here . . . I . . . please, Tony . . . just tell me what you remember.

Tony: Well of course. It was at that barbecue. After the run. We'd all changed and gone over across the field and she was there and you introduced us . . .

Scene Ten

Tony, Edgar, Alex approach Janine.

Alex: Aha, here she is. Fellas, this is my wife Janine. Janine, Tony . . .

Janine: *Shaking his hand.* Tony.

Tony: It's nice to meet you.

Alex: And Edgar . . .

Janine: Hi, yes, Edgar. *Shaking his hand.* You're the musician?

Edgar: That's right. You can tell by looking?

Janine: Actually, I remembered that the musician was the one with the kind of dashing name. *To Tony.* Oh, no offence.

Tony: None taken. You're completely right. Edgar's a great name. I covet it.

Edgar: I didn't know that.

Alex: I suppose we were all dashing today.

Tony: Yes, except everyone always runs so slowly at these things.

Alex: Well, it isn't really a race, so . . .

Edgar: But five people at the front always seem to think

that it is. Everyone else runs slower, so they don't get mistaken for that type of person.

Janine: Do you think maybe the people in front just want to be done as soon as possible?

Tony: You think they don't like running?

Janine: Not everyone does. Alex for example –

Alex: Janine!

Edgar: What?

Tony: First we've heard of that.

Alex: I'm sorry. I've been known to express . . . in the privacy of my home . . . an occasional lack of enthusiasm for this sport. But I always get past it.

Janine: Which is the whole running thing, right? The wall? Getting past the wall? Or over it?

Edgar: I think you're supposed to go through it.

Janine: That doesn't seem very pleasant. Or is there a door?

Edgar: I don't know. I guess I'm a simple sort of athlete. Does anyone want hot dogs? I think they're giving them out for free over there.

Alex: Oh hey, I'd go for one. Janine?

Janine: No thanks.

Alex: You're sure? They're free.

Janine: I wouldn't want one even if they were expensive. I'll take a glass of wine, though.

Alex: Sure, I'll get that. Tony? Hot dog? Wine? Beer?

Tony: I'm good, thanks.

Alex: Alright. *To Edgar.* You're coming, or –

Edgar: Of course. I'm particular about my toppings.

Alex: We'll be right back. Oh . . . Janine, red or white wine?

Janine: Red, please.

Edgar and Alex exit.

I haven't had a glass of white wine since 1995.

Tony: Oh? Bad experience?

Janine: It was the last date I went on before I met Alex. One of those types who orders everything for you.

Tony: Some see that as a romantic gesture.

Janine: Getting me something I don't want?

Tony: Wanting something on your behalf. Thinking that the list of things that might please you shouldn't be a finite one.

Janine: *After a little pause.* Alright, I hear you. But I remember the individual in question, and I think you've been a little overgenerous. The choice of wine wasn't really a dealbreaker.

Tony: Because there was no deal?

Janine: Exactly. *Pause.* So you're Tony. Mysterious Tony.

Tony: Oh? How's that?

Janine: Just . . . Oh, I don't even know. I shouldn't have –

Tony: Well, I guess I know what Alex thinks of me.

Janine: Well, I wouldn't make a big deal out of it. People often seem mysterious when you don't know them very well.

Tony: I guess that's as it should be.

Janine: I think he's just baffled by the notion of your not having to work. That's you, right? Independently wealthy?

Tony: I don't know what that means, exactly. I'm well set up from the sale of a successful family business.

Janine: But you don't depend on a job.

Tony: No, but I'm utterly dependent on my money.

Janine: I'm sorry. This conversation has taken a hugely personal turn.

Tony: It's alright. It's not like you asked for exact figures.

Janine: I wouldn't do that.

Tony: Because it's rude?

Janine: Of course. Is there any other reason to refrain?

Tony: Maybe because you'd rather speculate endlessly on what those figures might be.

Janine: What? Who thinks that way?

Tony: Maybe just me.

Janine: Ah. Pause. So then it stands to reason that . . . No, that's another personal thing. I mustn't.

Tony: Oh go on. You know you want to.

Janine: Yes and it's rude to introduce a topic and then renege.

Tony: It is. It's –

Janine: Despicable?

Tony: It's hard on a conversation.

Janine: Alright then . . . I was going to say . . . ask . . . if the reason you're still single is that you prefer imagining the myriad possibilities of who you might marry, to actually having to make a choice.

Tony: Sure, I'll cop to that. I don't see it as a form of stasis, though. Considering the myriad possibilities isn't done entirely inside one's head.

Janine: Of course not. But tell me you don't disapprove of marriage.

Tony: Certainly I don't. I'll bet the rewards are infinite.

Janine: Are you . . . being sarcastic?

Tony: No.

Janine: Oh. I'm sorry.

Tony: It's okay. Maybe I seem a little deadpan.

There's a pause.

Janine: I'm afraid to speak now.

Tony laughs. She looks at him.

Tony: Oh . . . you really meant that.

She continues to look at him. He doesn't look away, and eventually makes a questioning gesture which causes her to turn. He looks off in another direction.

Well . . . here comes Alex, so everything's going to be fine.

Janine: Thank God. And look . . . he brought me white wine.

Alex and Edgar enter with hot dogs and glasses of wine.

Alex: Here we are.

Edgar: Exercise has its benefits, finally.

Janine: *Taking the wine from Alex.* Yes, the years just fall away.

Alex: Oh, if only it were that easy.

Janine: *After sipping.* Mmm . . . chardonnay . . .

Alex: Oh crap. You wanted red.

Janine: I only thought I did.

She smiles. Alex and Edgar laugh politely. The light fades slowly, lingering on Janine as the men return to the coffee shop setting.

Scene Eleven

Alex, Edgar, and Tony, as before.

Alex: So that was it? That's the only time you ever saw her. Tony?

Tony: It was. It was an unusual conversation. Awkward, but not unpleasant. I didn't dwell on it particularly.

Alex: Right, well. I guess you're the one that didn't and she's the one that did.

Tony: What?

Alex: *Taking a pile of papers out of the envelope in front of him.* Take a look at these.

Tony: What are they? Letters?

Alex: They are. They're love letters. Passionate outpourings. There's a hundred and twenty-eight of them. Some are short, some go on for pages, and they're all addressed to you.

Tony picks up the top letter, looks at it, and puts it down.

Tony: Where did you find them?

Alex: In a box. In the closet where her shoes used to be.

Tony: And you've read them? All of them?

Alex: The first couple. Then I glanced at a few more. I can't really . . . They're not addressed to me.

Tony: You don't think that I . . . That she and I . . .

Alex: I sure don't want to.

Tony: Oh Alex, no. I don't know anything about this. I never talked to her or saw her after that one day.

Alex: Well . . . Flatly. That's such good news.

Tony: I'm sorry.

Alex: For what?

Tony: I don't know.

Alex: It's okay. I'll take your pity just the same. And you can have these. Maybe there are answers galore here, but I'm never gonna –

Tony: No, I'm not going to read them. They may be addressed to me, but she never sent them. She didn't intend for me to have them.

Edgar: Why would she leave something like this behind? A collection of incriminating documents?

Alex: I guess it was just one other thing she was done with. Standing. I'll let you dispose of them. Or keep them if you want. I'm going to go. I'm glad we got to talk about this, but I'm probably not going to see you guys for a while.

Tony: That's okay. Take the time you need.

Edgar: We're not going anywhere.

Alex: Yeah, me too.

He exits.

Edgar: Well that was . . . remarkable . . . What do you think –

Tony: I don't have an opinion.

Edgar: What do you want to do with these?

Tony: I don't want them. Throw them out. I don't even want to touch them.

Edgar: But this is an important record of something.

Tony: Take it then.

Edgar: But I'll read them if I take them. I know I will.

Tony: Maybe that's okay. Here's an idea . . . Pushing letters at Edgar. You just solve this and then don't tell me how you did it.

Edgar: Fine.

Tony: See ya.

Edgar: Bye-bye.

Tony exits. Light fades and Edgar exits with the letters.

Scene Twelve

Tony and Edgar return to the coffee shop, now in jackets to denote the coming of cooler weather. As lights come up, Tony is sitting at a table. Edgar enters.

Edgar: Hey, hi, here I am!

Tony: Edgar! Good to see you!

Edgar: Well, welcome home! I've missed you.

Tony stands and they embrace briefly.

Tony: That coffee's for you. I hope you want it.

Edgar: Of course I do. Sitting. So . . . and . . . Europe? It's all still there?

Tony: Pretty much. I ended up going to fewer places than I thought I would. Just France and Northern Italy, and then Switzerland for the marathon.

Edgar: Right, and that was in –

Tony: Interlaken.

Edgar: Was it hard? Running in the Alps? I guess Heidi did it a lot.

Tony: She'd need quite the constitution to do it for extended periods. A lot of going up steep inclines while breathing thin air.

Edgar: But then you'd get to run down, at least.

Tony: Funny thing. The view was always so great on the downward slopes that you couldn't help but go slower to enjoy it. It was like that for everyone. I've never seen so much walking in a marathon.

Edgar: Might be a good one for me, then. So what else? Where did you go in France?

Tony: Oh, a few places. I'll get to all that. I just . . . Something happened, at the end . . . On my way home . . . I was in Zurich, catching a flight to Frankfurt . . . and I met Janine.

Edgar: What? Janine? Alex's Janine? Who loved you?

Tony: Yeah. In the airport. In the Zurich airport.

Edgar: What was she doing there? She wasn't . . . Was she following you?

Tony: Stalking me? No, she wasn't. She had a pretty impeccable reason for being there.

Scene Thirteen

Tony crosses to another part of the stage, picking up a carry-on bag along the way. Janine approaches pulling a small suitcase. She's wearing a flight attendant uniform. They notice one another and stop in their tracks.

Tony: My God. Janine!

Janine: Tony! You're in Zurich.

Tony: Yeah, briefly. I'm just . . . catching a flight. Obviously.

Janine: Me too. It's what I do now. Indicating her uniform. Obviously.

Tony: You're a flight attendant?

Janine: I am. It's not exactly a new thing. It's what I always did. Before I was married.

Tony: Oh, okay. I never . . . knew that.

Janine: Well I guess . . . Uh . . .

Tony: It's good to see you, Janine.

Janine: Yes, and you.

He extends a hand and she makes to embrace him, and they choose the latter, hastily.

Tony: I . . . we wonder about you from time to time.

Janine: I'm sure Alex knows what I'm doing. We've had to be in touch a little. Because of the divorce.

Tony: Of course. I just haven't seen him. I did. Edgar and I did and then . . . Janine, have you got a moment? Can we sit?

Janine: I think . . . *Looking at her watch.* Yes. I'm fine for a few minutes.

Tony: Should we go somewhere? Get something . . .

Janine: I'd like to sit here, if that's alright. In the open.

Tony: Of course.

They move to seats and sit down.

Thanks for this.

Janine: It's alright. But if you're wanting to tell me something about Alex, I really don't need or want to hear –

Tony: It's not so much that. He's involved, obviously, but –

Janine: Oh. Okay. *Pause.* I know what it is.

Tony: Of course you do. He found your letters. The ones you wrote to me.

Janine: Did he read them?

Tony: No. He saw what they were and so he gave them to me.

Janine: And you read them?

Tony: No. You didn't give them to me, so I didn't read them.

Janine: And where are they now?

Tony: I don't know. In the wind.

Janine: Good. But I sense you still want to ask something.

Tony: Why would you leave them behind?

Janine: Well, I knew I wouldn't ever want to read them again. And yet I thought they might explain something to someone. Someday.

Tony: A hundred and twenty-eight letters, Janine. And you never sent one of them.

Janine: No. I planned to at the beginning. I wrote that first one about five times. At first I thanked you for the insightful things you had to say at the barbecue, and then I invited you to talk further on those topics, and then I told you I couldn't stop thinking about you, and then I said I had to see you again or I'd go crazy. And then I imagined your response. I realized you were probably the sort of decent person who wouldn't begin an affair with the wife of a friend. The fact that you haven't read those letters tells me I was probably right.

Tony: I'd say so, yes.

Janine: And then I remembered that the thing you'd said that sent me over the edge in the first place was something about enjoying oneself in a state of possibility. So I decided to do that.

I had an affair with you on paper. I shared my every thought in those letters. I wrote about my life and my choices and why I thought these would be of interest to you, given the way you perceived things. I went through every conceivable emotion and every degree of happiness and misery. And I always chose to imagine that you received my letters with enormous pleasure, so I continued for quite some time, until my way of seeing the world had evolved considerably. I realized that I didn't want to have an affair with you or marry you or possess you in any way. I just wanted to be as you are. That was all. So I stopped writing.

And then I knew I had to leave everything in my life and start again, and this was so terrifying to me that I went a little crazy. I tried to have an affair with my husband because I was afraid of what would happen to me if I walked away, the way my heart and my mind were telling me to. Doing that was definitely a mistake.

She laughs a little. He does too.

Tony: You think?

Janine: I know how selfish I look in all of this, but you have to believe me it was much worse before. There's no one who isn't better off now. Pause. You're not disagreeing?

Tony: No. Pause. You think . . . you are as I am? Is that what you said?

Janine: I think I am as I choose to believe you to be. I don't think it's a thing we can ever discuss.

Tony: Good. Great.

Janine: What are you doing in Zurich anyway?

Tony: I was in a marathon. In Interlaken.

Janine: Oh, nice. I've been running a bit myself, and I do mean literally. I've laced up in many of the world's great cities. It's a pretty exhilarating way to sight-see. Sometimes I'll pass beautiful mountains and lakes though, and get just a little annoyed because I don't own them. So you see I'm still working through a few things.

Tony: I suppose everyone is.

Janine: Exactly. *Looking at her watch.* And I should go. Off to London, then . . . I don't know. Halifax?

Tony: Well, thank you for this. I'm glad I saw you.

Janine: Yes. I didn't mind it at all.

She stands. He follows suit.

You look good, Tony. Really good.

Tony: Well, thank you. So do –

Janine: You look as good as I said you did in those letters.

Tony: Janine, don't –

Janine: Credit where it's due.

Tony: Okay, thanks.

Janine: I doubt I'll see you again, Tony, so I'd like you to kiss me good-bye.

Tony: Oh. Alright.

Janine: Just for the sake of . . . everything that was ever possible in the world.

Tony: Okay.

He steps toward her. They kiss, lingeringly.

Janine: Thank you.

Tony: Mm-hm.

Janine: Good-bye Tony.

Tony: Good-bye Janine.

She takes the handle of her luggage and walks away briskly. He stands a minute and then sits abruptly, clutching his suitcase. He breathes in and out a few times slowly, then regains his composure. He gets up and walks away.

Scene Fourteen

Having deposited his luggage, Tony returns to the coffee shop and sits with Edgar, as before.

Edgar: That's astonishing. I guess France kind of pales by comparison.

Tony: Good cheese, great wine, but . . . yeah. It's all pretty hokey once you've broken up in the Zurich airport with a woman you never even dated.

Edgar: So it was satisfying? There was a finality to it?

Tony: That kiss will haunt me all my life!

Edgar: As it should. Yes?

Tony: You think?

Edgar: A good kiss? Definitely. Everyone has to be haunted by something. Better that than, say, the lady that used to live in your apartment.

Tony: Fine. But you know . . . I think I could read those letters now.

Edgar: I don't know that that's a good idea.

Tony: So they still exist? You've got them somewhere. Have you read them?

Edgar: I've managed not to.

Tony: I want to see them. Again. Once. I think that's all.

Edgar: I guess. It's not really my call. It'll take a day or two.

Tony: I don't suppose there's a rush.

Edgar: But get on it tomorrow?

Tony: That'd be great.

Light fades and they exit.

Scene Fifteen

Edgar approaches Cora at her bank wicket.

Edgar: Good morning, Cora!

Cora: Edgar! Long time no see!

Edgar: Well, no one much studies the clarinet over the summer. No students means no cheques, but fall's here now, so I'll be a regular again soon.

Cora: Wonderful. And is there something I can help you with today?

Edgar: Actually, I'm here to get something from a safe deposit box.

Cora: Oh you know, you have to see Joanne about that, round the corner there.

Edgar: Yes, I know. I just wanted to say hello.

Cora: Oh, well, that's so nice. And I'm still hoping you'll let me know about your concerts. I'd love to give one another try.

Edgar: Well we're playing on Sunday afternoon, if you're not busy. Same church. Two o'clock.

Cora: Oh, that sounds doable.

Edgar: I don't have any tickets on me, but just come to the door. It's still free.

Cora: You should put out a donation basket.

Edgar: That's a good idea, and I'll suggest it. Coming from a banker, it might have some weight.

Cora: Good. I'll bring a little cash. I may even bring a friend.

Edgar: Fantastic!

Cora: Have a nice day!

He exits.

Scene Sixteen

At the church, after the concert. Tony is standing and looking at a programme leaflet. Alex and Cora enter.

Alex: Oh, Tony, hi!

Tony: Oh, Alex! And –

Alex: Cora.

Tony: Yes, that's right. We met here. Briefly. Once. You work at the bank.

Cora: That's right. Wasn't it a great concert? I'm so glad we came back.

Alex: Were you here the whole time?

Tony: I was in the balcony.

Cora: So you came in late?

Tony: No, I just like it better. Sound's always best in the cheap seats.

Cora: So much to learn.

Alex: And here's the man of the hour. Edgar!

Edgar: *Entering, carrying a paper bag with handles.* Hello! Look who all's here!

Tony: Good work there, chum.

Edgar: Thanks. And look, Alex is here. You came with Tony?

Alex: No no.

Cora: I brought him. It only took a little convincing.

Alex: For non-musical reasons, of course.

Edgar: Understandably.

Alex: But I'm so glad I did. So glad. I really enjoyed that.

Edgar: Well, good. Good. So . . . you two have . . . kept in touch.

Alex: You might say that.

Cora: We've been out and about a bit. Doing various activities.

Alex: We went camping.

Edgar: *Laughing.* Camping? Alex, I didn't realize you even –

Alex: Well, I didn't do it. For years.

Edgar: Well, this is great. That's wonderful.

Alex: We're going for coffee now, around the corner. Maybe you'll join us?

Tony: Sure, that sounds good. Edgar?

Edgar: Absolutely. Tony and just have to . . . talk about a little thing. Then we'll be right there.

Alex: Perfect.

Cora: We'll get a table.

Edgar: See ya there.

Alex and Cora exit. Edgar looks after them.

Is that our doing?

Tony: I think it must be, in a way.

Edgar: I'm so pleased.

Tony: So . . . we have to talk about a little thing.

Edgar: Right, yes. Well, it's not so much that as . . . I have a gift for you.

Tony: Really?

Edgar: Yup. Here ya go.

He takes out a gift box with a ribbon wrapped around it.

Tony: Oh, is this . . . Taking it and shaking it a bit. No . . . it doesn't weigh enough. Hardly anything.

Edgar: Maybe it's jewelry.

Tony: I'll just open it, shall I?

Edgar: Please.

Tony unties the ribbon and opens the box. He fishes around in the packing material.

Tony: I can't find anything.

Edgar: Keep fishin'.

Tony: Pulling out tufts. There's a lot of this stuff. Do you own a shredder?

Edgar: Yes.

Tony: Oh, I didn't know tha –. . . Oh.

Edgar: *After a pause.* I hope you're not disappointed.

Tony: You did all of them?

Edgar: Yes, though this is just a portion. There's a lot of bulk generated in shredding. *Pause.* Better say something.

Tony: Yes. Edgar . . . you are . . . a terribly good friend to me.

Edgar: Well, it's just because you're that to me. I thought . . . as much as I know you like to keep every possible ball in the air . . . as long as those letters existed, there was no way you could ever be completely happy.

Tony: Yes. Though I seem to remember that we once decided that was an unlikely prospect for just about everyone. Complete happiness. I don't expect it.

Edgar: Right. No one is going to be happy right down to the toes. We accepted that. But I have given that some thought and I think what might be possible is a kind of happiness that goes from the toes up.

Tony: That's interesting. Yes. Happiness can't start in the head. It's so hard for it to dominate, what with everything else that's there . . . But if it begins in the toes . . .

Edgar: It goes up. It nourishes and hydrates, like water absorbed through the roots of a great oak.

Tony: I like that notion. Happy from the toes up.

Edgar: Or just happy to be happy in the toes. You'd have a spring in your step, regardless of any other afflictions you might be enduring. I think I could live that way. Maybe I already do, though I certainly want as much happiness as I can get.

Tony: But as a worst-case scenario –

Edgar: Happy toes will see you through.

Tony: It makes sense.

Edgar: It's hard to talk about this and not also want to walk.

Tony: Then let's do it.

They walk, amusedly, to music. Alex and Cora enter and walk behind them, followed by Janine, also walking jauntily and pulling her suitcase. As they circle the stage, the light fades. Happily.

THE OCULIST'S HOLIDAY

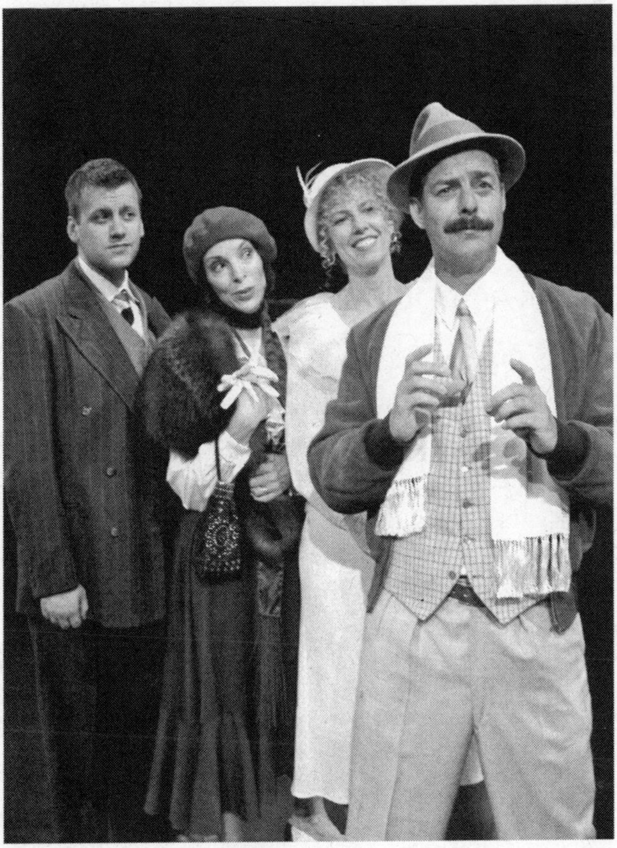

Mat Busby as Ted Fletcher, Davina Stewart as Laurette Hastings, Barbara Gates Wilson as Marian Ogilvy, Jeff Haslam as Charlie Hastings in *The Oculist's Holiday* (photo by Gina Moe)

PRODUCTION HISTORY

The Oculist's Holiday was first performed by Teatro La Quindicina in August of 2009, at the Varscona Theatre in Edmonton. It was part of the Edmonton International Fringe Theatre Festival.

CAST

Marian Ogilvy – Barbara Gates Wilson
Ted Fletcher – Mat Busby
Princess Volodevsky (Dorrie) – Leona Brausen
Charlie Hastings – Jeff Haslam
Laurette Hastings – Davina Stewart

Director – Stewart Lemoine
Costume Designer – Leona Brausen
Lighting Designer – Bobby Smale
Set Designer – Jeff Haslam
Stage Manager – Gina Moe

CHARACTERS

Marian Ogilvy – a Canadian teacher, in her early forties
Ted Fletcher – an American optometrist, in his thirties
Princess Volodevsky (Dorrie) – an American innkeeper, in her early fifties
Charlie Hastings – an American traveler, in his forties
Laurette Hastings – his wife, late thirties to early forties

SETTING

The Oculist's Holiday takes place principally in Lausanne, Switzerland in 1931 and 1934. Marian's framing graduation address takes place in Toronto in 1934.

In the premiere production, the terrace of the Maison de la Princesse was a permanent location at upstage centre, comprised of two tables, each with a pair of chairs, and a sideboard. All other scenes took place on either side of the stage, with basic furniture pieces set in front of revolving panels covered with enlarged period photographs, evocative of the various locations.

MUSIC

The incidental music heard in *The Oculist's Holiday* consisted primarily of excerpts from the *Piano Trio #1* by Felix Mendelssohn (1809–1847). It's an elegant yet often urgent work of poised intensity, and excerpts from the outer movements were heard at the start of the play and in scene transitions. The exquisite beginning to the slow second movement was featured at three moments, all linked to the notion of the holiday from which one doesn't return: first, underscoring Dorrie's reminiscence of Doctor Wilmer Jarvis; second, as Marian crosses to complete her address to the graduates following her dismissal of Ted in the train station; and third, underscoring the conclusion of the final conversation between Charlie and Laurette and playing out during the final fadeout when she's left him alone.

Marian and Charlie's scene at the bar in the Palace Hotel was also underscored by the distant sound of a jazz orchestra playing appropriate selections of the period.

THE OCULIST'S HOLIDAY

Prologue

Toronto, 1934. Marian Ogilvy stands centre stage in a tightly lit area.

Marian: Good afternoon, ladies. It's a pleasure to speak to you today and wish you well as 1934's graduates of this fine institution. As Mrs. Williams said in her opening remarks, a diploma from the Southern Ontario Business College for Women is not an end in itself, but rather a beginning. It's something that will enable you to take your place in a world in which there are rapidly increasing opportunities and possibilities for our gender. There is more waiting for you than simply secretarial work, and I hope that you're not just now hearing this for the first time.

She smiles and looks over the audience.

I suppose I was asked here so that I could tell you of some of my experiences as an independent-minded woman who has been consistently employed for the better part of two decades. That'd be absorbing for some and maybe a little tedious for others, but I really don't feel it'd be appropriate for me to inspire you *or* to bore you, because I feel instead such a profound need to warn you about something. It has to do with the way you live your life, whether it be at work or at play, at home, or in an office. And in order to make my point, I'm going to tell you all a little story, not about an experience that's related to employment, but rather to a holiday I once took. Yes?

It was just three years ago, and after a few weeks traveling thither and yon in Europe, I found myself somewhat unexpectedly in the small Swiss city of Lausanne, which sits picturesquely on a slope on the shores of Lake Geneva. Arriving without a hotel reservation, I was directed by a concierge at the train station toward a lovely guesthouse called Maison de la Princesse, which was run by a curious sort of noblewoman of mixed pedigree.

Light comes up a little on a small outdoor terrace at Maison de la Princesse, where Dorrie is setting out breakfast things.

For a while, it appeared I would be the only guest, but later in the afternoon, a young American man also checked in.

Ted appears on the terrace and exchanges a few words with Dorrie.

We nodded politely in passing, but didn't speak until later, when we both found ourselves alone in the bar at the Lausanne Palace Hotel. We had a few champagne cocktails and some other local drink specialties, then discovered a jazz orchestra playing in an adjacent salon, where we danced and had a few more cocktails and then made our way back to the house of the Princess, where we retired swiftly to my room.

Pause. The hotel setting fades.

Ladies, please . . . Whatever your excited murmurs are about, I can assure you they're less interesting than what I'm trying to relate. Mrs. Thompson, I see you getting up to leave and I'm recommending that you don't. If you're going to continue teaching young women, you really ought to hear what I have to say. Looking to one side. I see your windmill gestures Mrs. Williams, and I'm not going to respond. The young ladies are quiet now, and I believe that means they'd like me to continue.

So . . . as I said, the young man . . . Well he was younger than me, but hardly a boy . . . he came back to my room and that went more or less as it does . . . and then there was, as there always is, a subsequent encounter under changed circumstances.

Scene One

Marian is sitting at a table with a cup of coffee. She's wearing dark glasses. Ted enters after a little, and Marian looks up at him.

Marian: Oh. Good morning.

Ted: Good morning. Pause. May I . . .

Marian: Indicating the other chair at her table. It should go without saying, I suppose. Though that principle never really works.

Ted: I think you're quite right.

He sets his cup down and sits.

Marian: Things that should go without saying should be said regardless, as they'll almost always be gratefully heard.

Ted takes a pair of sunglasses from his breast pocket and puts them on.

You should know . . . I'm not trying to bore you on purpose. It's just happening all on its own.

Ted: I'm not bored. Just the opposite, actually.

Marian: Oh-oh.

She takes a sip of her coffee. There's a pause.

I suppose I should thank you for slipping away so quietly last night.

Ted: You aren't mad?

Marian: Heavens, no. Imagine the alternatives.

He smiles, nods, and takes a sip of coffee.

The lake is beautiful this morning. Such clear skies, too. It seems a shame to view them through any sort of filter.

She raises her glasses and squints a bit into the distance. He does the same.

Ted: Yes, that really is extraordinary.

They look at each other for a moment. She lowers her glasses.

Marian: But a little too much at this hour.

Ted: Lowering his glasses. I agree. And it's just practical, really. A little filtration now and we won't be peering through cataracts later in life.

Marian: Yes, my thoughts exactly. Pause. May I just add that practicality and sensibility are generally quite important to me, so it was definitely a bit of an aberration when I – . . . succumbed . . .

Ted: To me? Is that how we're remembering it?

Marian: No, that wouldn't be quite right, would it. I succumbed to champagne and then to . . . what was it . . . slivovitz?

Ted: They call it pruneau here, but it's pretty much that. Plum brandy.

Marian: Pruneau? Well, good for you for remembering.

Ted: I guess if you order anything enough times . . .

Marian: Yes, and really, I'm sorry to have raised the notion of anyone succumbing to anything. The pleasures of last evening would only be compromised by our attributing them to any sort of weakness.

Ted: Don't blame the intoxicants?

Marian: Precisely. They were as intoxicating as we wanted them to be.

Ted: But you're still glad I left before you awoke.

Marian: I think I have to be. And it's because what I have to say to you now will maybe be a little less awkward than it would have been if we were still lying in bed together.

Ted: Oh-oh. That sounds dire.

Marian: It doesn't have to be. If you maintain a sense of humour about it.

Ted: Alright, I'll try. Let me have it.

Marian takes off her sunglasses. He does the same. She reaches across the table and touches his hand.

Marian: I don't remember your name.

Ted: Oh . . .

Marian: Please don't be angry.

Ted: I'm not. I couldn't be . . . because . . .

He smiles awkwardly.

Marian: You don't . . . Oh, that's such a relief.

Ted: Is it? Good. Pause. So, I'm –

Marian: No no, let's linger in the moment for a bit. There'll never be another like it.

Dorrie enters, carrying a basket of pastries.

Dorrie: Aha, the guests are getting acquainted.

Marian: We are, after a fashion. Good morning, Princess.

Dorrie: It's a good morning, indeed. I have some pastries here, just now delivered. Scrumptious.

She sets the basket on the table.

Help yourselves. Eat all you want. You were my only guests last night, as it turned out, so we've brioche and croissants and what-have-you in great abundance, and they'll just go stale.

Ted: Taking a pastry. Well, we don't want that.

Dorrie: We certainly don't. I'm so glad to see you sitting together. Some days the place is just plumb full of guests and I find them all out sitting by themselves, staring off at the lake and pretending for some reason that they're not all having the same experience.

Marian: Surely you don't think they're all thinking identical thoughts, Princess.

Dorrie: No, of course not, and if that isn't a good incentive for conversation, I don't know what would be. I'll admit to being gregarious in nature, though. Winking at Ted. That's opened a lot of doors for me.

Ted: Or maybe it's helped you open a lot of doors for yourself.

Dorrie: Yes yes, very clever. It has. Even now, I see the two of you here and I'm compelled to sit down for a bit, and yet . . . that might not be what's appropriate, so –

Marian: Princess, please, I think we'd be delighted.

Dorrie: Yes?

Ted: Of course. *Getting a chair from an adjoining table.* You must join us.

Dorrie: Alright then. I've just a couple of things to attend to in the kitchen, and I'll be right back. I'm so pleased. Thrilled even. *Bowing slightly to each in turn.* Dr. Fletcher. Mrs. Ogilvy.

She exits. They watch her go, then turn to each other.

Marian: Doctor.

Ted: Mrs. *Pause.* I suppose there'll never be another moment like this one either.

Marian: *After a pause.* I'm a widow.

Ted: I see. Good.

Marian: You're pleased. That I –

Ted: I'm sorry for your loss, of course. I'm just glad you don't have a living husband lurking, and if that's a terrible thing to say, well I'm sorry for that too.

Marian: You know, I think I'm managing to hear it as a compliment. And I suppose I did withhold the information somewhat.

Ted: He died recently?

Marian: No. Fifteen years ago. In France.

Ted: Ah. In the war?

Marian: That's right.

Ted: Then I'm truly sorry. That must be the worst sort of loss.

Marian: Yes, and you know, we were married just three years and were never particularly happy. You might think that would make widowhood a bit easier to take, but initially, it didn't do that. With age comes perspective though, and a sort of quiet certainty that I'd probably have been a divorcee by now if things hadn't gone the way they did.

Ted: And yet you maintain the respectability of a . . . no, I'll leave that thought unexpressed.

Marian: I hear you though. And as long as we're withdrawing observations, I could wish that I hadn't mentioned the notion of age just now.

Ted: And yet you've done it again.

Marian: Time for an abrupt change of topic. Doctor . . . Doctor Fletcher . . . please tell me you aren't a veterinarian.

Ted: I'm not. I'm an optometrist.

Marian: Really?

Ted: Yes. Is there a reason that's particularly surprising?

Marian: There shouldn't be, given that you mentioned cataracts earlier. Oh, now here comes her majesty.

Ted: Quietly. Is she really a princess?

Marian: It seems so. I predict we're about to find out the details.

Ted: Why's that?

Marian: Mostly because of the questions you're going to ask her.

He raises his eyebrows.

Challenge, as the locals might say.

Dorrie enters with a cup and saucer. She sets it down and picks up a coffee pot from the table.

Dorrie: Let me just top you up a little.

Ted: Standing. No no, I won't have it. Taking the pot. I won't sit and have a princess pour my coffee. It'll be my pleasure and my honor to fill your cup, madame.

Dorrie: Oh, but it really isn't –

Ted: Please. I mean business.

Dorrie: Well then, I thank you, Doctor.

She sits. Marian offers her the basket of baking.

Marian: Brioche?

Dorrie: I don't mind if I do. But really, when I invited myself to your table, it wasn't my intention to have you wait on me.

Ted: I think it's how it ought to be here at Maison de la Princesse. In exchange for the hospitality and reasonably priced lodgings you provide, guests can experience a unique taste of life as the servants of a noblewoman. For that's what you are, if I'm correct?

Dorrie: I hardly know what it means to be noble, Doctor Fletcher, but I do have a title. I'm the Princess Volodevsky. Dorrie to my friends. I suppose I don't quite make sense to you.

Ted: I'm not sure I'd have things otherwise.

Dorrie: Oh, but you're curious, so I'll tell. I was born and raised in Indiana. I moved to New York City and became a chorus girl. Did that for a few years, then traveled to Paris with a revue. I married a Russian prince and we swanned around Europe for a couple of years. Then things began to change in his homeland and he decided he'd go back and settle some financial affairs, which was of course a terrible idea. I was to wait for him here, and he never returned.

Ted: And you think –

Dorrie: No, I know exactly what happened. He was executed, Doctor Fletcher. So many of them were.

Marian: I'm so sorry, Princess.

Dorrie: Please, Dorrie really is what I prefer, among friends.

Marian: And so . . . Dorrie you've just stayed on here ever since?

Dorrie: Yes, of course. I had no plans of any sort, no family back home, really. My performing gifts were modest, to say the least. But I had a lot of jewels and a decent amount of my husband's money in the bank here, so I started anew. I love Lausanne. We were actually headed for Geneva and the train stopped here and I looked out and said, "Oh darling, I think I'm home."

Marian: You know, that's exactly what happened to me yesterday. I was going to Geneva too. I had a hotel booked and everything. I didn't think I was home, exactly. But I couldn't not have a look.

Dorrie: And you, Doctor Fletcher?

Ted: I was going the other way. To Zurich, but yes.

Dorrie: So many of my guests are surprised to be here. It keeps a little edge of excitement in the house, which is a blessing a in a quiet town. You're both traveling freely in Europe? It seems?

Marian: I have been. I'm sailing home from Naples in just a few days.

Dorrie: And home is . . .

Marian: Canada. Toronto.

Dorrie: And you have a career of some sort that you're returning to?

Marian: I suppose I do. I'm an editor of textbooks. For grade schools. I devised the current system by which Ontario's children learn to spell.

Dorrie: And how is that working?

Marian: Oh, I'm afraid to ask. I moved on to other things. Six months ago I was preparing a geography manual and suddenly became profoundly embarrassed by the fact that I'd never been anywhere outside of North America.

Dorrie: Aha, and now you've rectified that.

Marian: Yes yes, with a vengeance.

Dorrie: And you, Doctor Fletcher, is it business or pleasure that brings you to Europe?

Ted: It's a sort of a mixture. I'm here to think, but what I'm thinking about is my profession.

Dorrie: Mm. No, that's not clear to me.

Ted: I'm possibly going to take over my father's practice back home in Ohio.

Dorrie: But you requested time and distance to think it over.

Ted: I didn't. He told me I had to go traveling or he wouldn't even consider giving it up to me.

Dorrie: A wise parent. It's a medical practice, obviously, Doctor?

Marian: He's an optometrist.

Dorrie: You're trained and qualified?

Ted: Completely.

Dorrie: But you're still having second thoughts?

Ted: Those are mainly about Ohio.

Dorrie: Yes, I hear you there. But wait, Doctor Fletcher . . . you're on an oculist's holiday. Would it be fair to say that?

Ted: If it were 1880, maybe. It's not exactly wrong, but the word's not used much, since ophthalmology and optometry are now largely differentiated fields and –

Dorrie: Yes, yes, I understand, but in broad terms it still might apply, and I have an interesting story to tell, so let's just buy in.

Ted: Of course.

Dorrie: You see . . . In the town where I grew up, there was an elderly eye doctor who had a practice right on the main street. He had a sign painted right in his window. *Dr. Wilmer Jarvis, Oculist.* And every summer for two weeks, there would be a smaller sign affixed to the door saying "Closed. The Oculist is on holiday."

My father always found this amusing. He wondered if an oculist's holiday would be different from a regular holiday in some way.

Marian: It'd be introspective, wouldn't you think? A holiday where one looks deep inside one's own head.

Ted: Or where one who normally does that would look outward to really comprehend all the things in the wide world that he was helping his patients to be able to see.

Dorrie: Well, those both make sense, but ultimately it came to mean something quite different to us, because one summer, Dr. Wilmer Jarvis, Oculist, just didn't come back. And yet the sign stayed up in the door window for years. "The Oculist is on holiday." My father decided conclusively that an oculist's holiday would henceforth be a holiday from which one simply never returned.

Ted: Well, if that's the case, then it's not what I'm on. I've a passage from Southampton to New York booked in a month.

Dorrie: Well, so much for that notion. I haven't really thought about it in years. My father was a wonderful man. Always amused by something. He'd have gotten such a kick out of my unexpected life.

She smiles thoughtfully, then frowns a little and looks from one to the other.

I'm quite capable of talking all day, jut so you know. Standing. You two should go do some sightseeing. Then in the evening, we'll discuss your findings. Sounds nice? Yes? Smiles all round? Enjoy your day.

She turns and exits.

Marian: Thank you, Princess. Dorrie.

Ted: We'll see you later.

Marian: Well, what do you think? Should we do as she says?

Ted: See some sights? Of Lausanne? I think I'd like that.

Marian: As they get up. Good. We should have a guidebook, probably.

Ted: She keeps some in the front parlour.

Marian: Oh, perfect. Perhaps you can read to me.

Ted: I can and will. I'm warning you, I'll mangle the French names rather badly.

Marian: But you'll make up for it with the Latin ones.

Ted: *Ut est verum quod tantum verum.*

Marian: Smiling. I'll get my hat.

Ted: Mrs. Ogilvy . . . my name is Ted.

Marian: Ted . . . my name is Marian.

She smiles and exits quickly, and he follows as lights fade.

Scene Two

Late afternoon. Dorrie is setting out some glasses and liquor bottles. Ted and Marian return.

Dorrie: Aha, home at last. You've seen many sights, I'm thinking.

Marian: We have, and now I'm thoroughly spent. This city sits on quite the rake.

Ted: Clearly the citizens of Lausanne are a strong-calved people.

Dorrie: To a point, yes. Others of us are artful at zigging and zagging. Did you see the cathedral?

Marian: We did. We climbed the tower too, which will take its toll later, but heavens, the view!

Dorrie: Is it so much better than this one?

Marian: Dorrie, I think it is.

Dorrie: Well I'll take your word for it.

Marian: We went to the park too, with the villa where . . . someone . . . lived.

Ted: Voltaire.

Marian: Yes, that's who it was. I envy the man his lodgings. Probably also his genius, but I can't say as I've read . . . Oh – oh. You're putting out liquor.

Dorrie: But of course. It's cocktail hour at the Maison de la Princesse.

Marian: Oh dear, I really wonder if that's a horse I should be getting back onto.

Dorrie: Do as you wish.

Marian: No no, you see, that's the problem. But I'm really just being tiresome. I've been walking for hours and a cocktail would be quite perfect.

Dorrie: That's the spirit.

Marian: But first I need to splash some water on my face and maybe down a little as well. *Looking at the table of drinks.* That's a generous number of glasses.

Ted: Someone else is expected, perhaps?

Dorrie: As a matter of fact, more guests have arrived. An American couple, on a driving holiday, it seems.

Marian: Oh, interesting.

Dorrie: Yes, though whether they join us for drinks is still a matter for conjecture. *Confidentially.* Just between us . . . no luggage.

Ted: Ooo.

Marian: Scandalous.

She gives Ted a bemused glance.

I'll be back momentarily. Maybe sooner.

She goes out.

Dorrie: Help yourself to whatever you like, Doctor Fletcher. I'll be back with some hors d'oeuvres.

Ted: Thanks, Dorrie.

She exits. Ted crosses and pours himself a small amount of whisky. He crosses down and looks off at the view. After a moment, Charlie and Laurette Hastings enter.

Charlie: Ah, here we are, Mrs. Hastings. Looks like the bar's open.

Laurette: Well, thank heaven.

Ted: Turning. Oh, good evening.

Charlie: Isn't it though? Striding forward and clasping Ted's hand. Charlie Hastings.

Ted: Charlie, I'm Ted Fletcher.

Charlie: Good to meet you, sir. The Princess mentioned there were Americans in the house.

Ted: Well, one. The other guest's actually a Canadian.

Charlie: Mmm, exotic.

Laurette: Charlie, I want a drink.

Charlie: My wife Laurette.

Laurette: What?

Charlie: Laurette, I'm introducing you to Mr. Fletcher. Come over here.

Laurette: *Crossing.* Oh, hello. I'm Laurette.

Ted: *Shaking her hand.* Ted.

Laurette: That sounds American.

Ted: And it is.

Laurette: Are you on a holiday?

Ted: I am. I'll be seeing what I can of Europe in the next several weeks.

Laurette: That's fun. We more or less live here.

Ted: Oh yes. You've a job here in Switzerland, Mr. Hastings?

Charlie: Hey, it's Charlie. And no. I'm here at my leisure.

Ted: Well, that's lucky.

Laurette: Am I getting a drink at all?

Charlie: Of course I'm not without obligations. Coming right up, darling. You just enjoy the view with Ted here.

Laurette: Alright. Don't forget to put ice in, though. You know how much I like it.

Charlie: I won't forget.

He crosses to the bar.

Laurette: Some places they don't give you any at all. They're stingy with it, which seems silly. It's a pretty cheap commodity, wouldn't you think?

Ted: Yes, especially here.

Laurette: Why's that?

Ted: Well because of . . . all the glaciers.

Laurette: Oh. *Laughing.* Right. *Pause.* So . . . the view . . . what are we looking at particularly?

Ted: Well . . . the lake. The expanse of it.

Laurette: Right. It is fairly big, isn't it? Compared to other lakes in other places. We were in Geneva and the lake there didn't seem as large as this one. And the lake they have in Montreux was maybe a bit bigger, but still not like this. I think.

Ted: Actually, they're all the same lake.

Laurette: Pardon me?

Ted: This is Lake Geneva. All three cities are on its shores.

Laurette: Well, how about that. So I'm right that it's a big one?

Ted: Absolutely.

Laurette: Charlie, did you know that this is the same lake as the one they have in Geneva?

Charlie: Yes, I guess I did.

Laurette: Well, you could have mentioned it.

Charlie: Sorry, darling.

Laurette: *To Charlie.* I'm not mad. *To Ted.* I just like to know things. And Charlie has a lot to keep track of. Driving, I mean. We're driving around in a car.

Ted: That sounds exciting.

Laurette: Oh, it is. It's nerve-wracking, but I guess I enjoy that.

Charlie approaches with a drink for Laurette and one for himself.

Charlie: Here you are, darling.

Laurette: Aha, at last. Sipping. Dear sweet Lillet. Well, bitter-sweet, really. That's a good thing. Keeps me from guzzling. Cheers, gentlemen.

Ted: Yes, cheers.

Charlie: Hip-hip.

They clink their glasses and drink. Marian enters, having changed into something a little more formal.

Marian: Oh my. A party is in full swing.

Charlie: Yes yes, it certainly is now, at any rate. This must be the distinguished Canadian visitor we've heard talk of.

Ted: It is she.

Charlie: Crossing to Marian, extending a hand. Charlie Hastings.

Marian: Advancing, shaking his hand. I'm Marian Ogilvy.

Charlie: Glad to meet you, Miss Ogilvy. Or Mrs.?

Marian: It's a little of both.

Charlie: Fascinating. Here's my wife Laurette.

Laurette: Poking at her ice. Beg pardon?

Charlie: I'm introducing you to Marian Ogilvy.

Laurette: Shaking Marian's hand. Then hello there.

Charlie: And of course you already know Ted.

Marian: I do. It's nice to see you again, Dr. Fletcher.

Ted: And you, Mrs. Ogilvy.

Marian: What's it been? Five minutes? Ten? To Charlie. We've just come back from sightseeing. Or maybe you already knew that.

Charlie: I didn't. And I'll bet you could use a drink.

Marian: Certainly. I wouldn't mind.

Charlie: My wife enjoys the Lillet.

Marian: Then I'm sure I will too.

Charlie goes to the bar and pours a drink.

Laurette: Hey, did I hear right? One of you's a doctor?

Ted: Yes, that'd be me.

Laurette: Well, what a disappointment.

Ted: It is?

Laurette: Sure, on account of your seeming like such a nice normal person.

Ted: You think I'm not?

Laurette: Oh, I don't know. I just don't generally care for –

Charlie: Laurette's a little distrustful of the medical profession. It's what keeps her so healthy.

Ted: Did you have a bad experience? Actually, don't answer that. If you did, I'm sure you don't want to talk about it.

Marian: I can be a bit of a nervous patient myself. But I assure you, no one has anything to fear from Dr. Fletcher. He's an optometrist.

Laurette: Well, that's good at least. A positive outlook.

Ted: After a pause. Yes.

Charlie: Returning with a drink for Marian. Here you are, Mrs. Ogilvy.

Marian: Please, Marian.

Charlie: Certainly, Marian.

Laurette: So, will Mr. Ogilvy be joining us?

Marian: Ah . . . no. Actually . . . I'm a widow.

Laurette: Oh! I'm sorry. I just can't seem to win tonight.

Marian: No no, I really should have said something. It's well in the past though, not to worry. Let's just be merry. Cheers!

All respond and raise glasses.

Oh, this Lillet is quite lovely. Much more my speed than that . . . what was it . . . the local plum hooch.

Ted: Pruneau.

Charlie: A bad experience? Oh but wait, you wouldn't want to talk about that.

Marian: Precisely. I hear you two are on a driving holiday. That sounds quite mad.

Charlie: Why do you say that?

Marian: Just so many cliffs and valleys in this part of the world.

Charlie: That's what makes it so exhilarating.

Ted: What sort of car are you driving, Charlie?

Charlie: It's a Stutz 8. Wouldn't want anything less with these elevations.

Marian: I rode round Lake Ontario in a Stutz Bearcat once.

Quite the pummeling we all took. I hope your car's not like that.

Charlie: They've made improvements, fortunately.

Laurette: My husband had a Stutz Bearcat. He loved it a lot more than he ever loved me.

Charlie: *After a little pause.* Laurette is referring to her brief first marriage.

Marian: I thought as much. More and more people seem to have had those.

Charlie: It's so true.

Marian: And of course another not-to-be-discussed experience. Come, let's sit. Laurette? Sit next to me here. Won't you?

Laurette: *With sudden affection.* I don't mind.

She takes Marian's arm. They cross and sit.

Ted: You'll have met the Princess, of course.

Charlie: We certainly did. Fascinating woman.

Marian: Rather a sad story, though she's ended up well.

Laurette: Why would you say that?

Marian: Well, because she seems happy in what she does.

Laurette: Still, she was a princess and now she runs a boarding house. I never heard of a fairy tale that ended like that.

Marian: I wouldn't exactly call this a boarding house.

Laurette: Well, it's not the Palace Hotel. Is it, Charlie?

Charlie: No, Laurette, and that's why we chose it.

Laurette: Friends of mine stayed there. At the Palace. They said it was beyond elegant.

Marian: And they were right. But a lot of those swank places seem rather similar after a while.

Charlie: That's what I think too. You're never alone in a big hotel like that.

Laurette: Well, we're not exactly alone here either. Oh . . . That sounded mean. I just meant . . . what's the difference? You're alone or you're not.

Marian: Yes. That's perfectly clear.

Dorrie enters with a tray of hors d'oeuvres.

Dorrie: Aha, everyone's here. And I've brought food for you at last.

Charlie: Princess, that's grand of ya.

Dorrie: I have blinis, freshly made, and to top them, there's a spread of chicken livers with capers, and also caviar.

Marian: Oh, very nice.

Ted: Very Russian, I think.

Dorrie: But of course.

Laurette: I don't suppose there's any cheese.

Dorrie: There isn't. I do serve cheese at breakfast.

Laurette: So you're saying there's some in the house?

Dorrie: I –

Charlie: Laurette, we can't expect the Princess to run and get us whatever we ask for.

Laurette: I thought we could. I thought that was the joke here.

Charlie: Not really. She's our hostess, but not our servant.

Laurette: Fine. Never mind. I just asked for a little cheese.

Dorrie: Mrs. Hastings, I don't mind. I'll go and –

Laurette: No, your majesty, please don't. Not if it makes me out to be a heel.

Dorrie: Please, it's just Dorrie. My name is Dorrie.

Laurette wrinkles her nose a little at this, but says nothing.

Ted: Ladies, let me get you some blinis. Yes?

Marian: Thanks, Ted.

Ted crosses to the table where Dorrie has laid out the food and puts some hors d'oeuvres on little plates.

Dorrie: Everyone's drinks are all right?

Marian: I think so. I'm enjoying this Lillet, which Laurette kindly recommended.

Dorrie: Yes, I like that too. Taking up the bottle. Perhaps I'll have a dram. Can I top you ladies up, while the bottle's open?

Laurette: Yes please.

Charlie takes a breath, but says nothing.

Were you going to say something, Charlie?

Charlie: No.

Laurette: That's too bad. To Marian. He usually likes it when I agree to have another. He always says so.

Dorrie pours a little Lillet into Laurette's glass.

Dorrie: Mrs. Ogilvy?

Marian: I'm fine right now, thanks Dorrie.

Dorrie crosses to the bar and pours herself a glass. Ted approaches the ladies with a small plate of food.

Ted: Here you go. A little plate for you to share.

Marian: *Taking it.* Thank you. Laurette. Will you have a blini?

Laurette: Oh, alright. *Quietly.* Say, Ted, I don't suppose I might ask you to slip a little more ice in my drink. I'd ask the hostess, but then we'd probably be at war with Russia.

Ted: It's no trouble, Laurette.

He takes her glass and crosses away.

Laurette: Now there's a gentleman. You'll want to hang on to him.

Marian: Oh, I . . . Yes,

Laurette takes a bite of her blini and grimaces a little.

Laurette: *Quietly.* Ugh! Caviar. It's so dreadful but you just have to pretend you like it if you're going to fit in anywhere. *Taking another bite.* Mmneh . . . That's one thing I really didn't miss.

Marian: Pardon me?

Laurette: I said I didn't . . . eat caviar . . . for a while.

Marian: After your divorce?

Laurette: Exactly.

Ted: *Handing Laurette her glass.* Here you are, Laurette.

Laurette: Oh, thanks. *Shaking it a little.* Oh, I do love that tinkle.

Marian: Will you try the liver?

Laurette: Marian, I won't.

Charlie: Well I'd like to propose a toast. To the Princess here, and her wonderful hospitality.

Dorrie: Oh, you're too kind.

Ted: Tell us, what would be an appropriate toast in Russian?

Dorrie: I only remember one. It's short . . . Za Vas!

Charlie: Perfect. Everyone . . .

All: Except Laurette. Za Vas!

They drink.

Laurette: Now Princess, you met your husband in Paris, was that right?

Dorrie: I did.

Laurette: There's a lot of Russian princes there, apparently.

Dorrie: Yes, more than ever nowadays.

Laurette: Only none of them have money anymore, that's what I've heard.

Dorrie: It's true, sadly.

Laurette: So you lucked out there, Dorrie.

Marian: Oh, Laurette!

Laurette: What, am I wrong?

Marian: No, just –

Ted: It's not just the princes, though. A lot of people don't have money anymore.

Laurette: What?

Ted: Since the stock market crash.

Laurette: Oh, let's not talk about that, please.

Ted: Another bad experience?

Laurette: No, it's just boring. We've got lots of money. Charlie, tell them how much you're worth.

Charlie: Laurette, I don't think –

Laurette: No, Charlie, it's such an impressive figure. It's something to be proud of.

Marian: Please, we're happy to use our imaginations.

Laurette: But if it's true that everyone's gone all poor, then I think it's all the more wonderful that someone would be worth over –

Charlie: Laurette, stop. Just drop this.

Laurette: Fine. *To Marian.* It was quite another thing when he wanted me to get in the car and head out on this ridiculous –

Charlie: Laurette!

Laurette: Charlie! What?

Charlie: I'm not sure your drink is agreeing with you.

Laurette: Oh, this one's alright. But one of the previous three you poured me upstairs might have been a mistake.

Charlie: Laurette, why don't you go on back to our room? You can lie down for a bit.

Laurette: Why don't I? Because I'm tired of that. I'm tired of lying down and resting! *Getting up.* If you want me gone, I'll leave, but I'll be going a lot further than upstairs.

Charlie: *Taking her arm.* Laurette –

Laurette: *Pushing him away.* Let go of me! Let me go!

Charlie: Alright, fine. Go for a walk. That might be a good idea too.

Laurette: Yeah, Charlie. It really might. Maybe I'll go swim in the big lake. Or better yet, maybe I'll find a bar where I can have a drink and not get judged for it.

She exits.

Charlie: I'm sorry. Sometimes she –

Marian: Of course. No need to apologize.

Ted: I really don't think she should be on the streets . . . alone.

Charlie: Well, my going after her is not going to help. *Pause.* But, I suppose –

Ted: No, I'll go. If that's easier.

Marian: Yes. If she doesn't know the city –

Ted: Exactly.

He exits quickly. There is a pause.

Charlie: Marian, Dorrie . . . I'm sorry you had to see that.

Marian: Don't be embarrassed. Not on my account. New surroundings, new people . . . It's easy to lose one's bearings on a holiday, even when everything's so pleasant.

Charlie: I shouldn't have let her drink so much.

Marian: That's never an easy call to make. You shouldn't have to be blaming yourself in instances like these.

Charlie: Well . . . thank you for saying so.

Dorrie: It doesn't hurt, though, to maybe take it as a lesson for the future.

Charlie: Duly noted, Princess.

Dorrie: *Picking up the tray of food.* These things shouldn't just sit out. I'll keep them cool and maybe people can enjoy them later.

Marian: Thanks Dorrie. That's probably best.

Dorrie goes inside. Marian gets up and crosses downstage. She peers into the distance for a bit, then turns to Charlie.

You really don't think you should go after her?

Charlie: I know it makes sense, but I can tell you, I just wouldn't know what I could say that might make things better. *Pause.* I guess we have a funny sort of a marriage.

Marian: Oh, I don't even know that that's true.

Charlie: And your friend Ted seems a stable, sympathetic type. She'll like that better than . . . well, any other type.

Marian: Probably, yes.

Charlie: I say your friend Ted, but he's not really, is he? I mean you're not acquaintances of long standing?

Marian: No, not really. We spent the day sightseeing, as I think I mentioned.

Charlie: That's nice. Laurette and I really don't do things like that.

Marian: Have you been married a long time, Charlie?

Charlie: No. A few months.

Marian: Well, it takes a while, doesn't it, to adjust to any sort of new arrangements.

Charlie: Sure it does. And we're not exactly kids either. We're used to doing things the way we do them.

Marian: And that can be a good and a bad thing.

Charlie: Yup.

Marian: You know, it's a little breezier here than I'd anticipated. I'm just going to step up to my room and get myself some sort of a wrap.

Charlie: You'll come back, though?

Marian: Oh, of course. We can't all abandon you. Oh, now that sounded –

Charlie: No, I appreciate it.

Marian: Good.

She exits. He smiles after her, then turns and looks off. Abruptly, he exhales sharply in frustration and sits down. He puts his head in his hand and presses his temples and pushes hard against his closed eyes. He reaches into his inside jacket pocket, takes out a small bottle and shakes out a few pills. He gets up and crosses to the bar and looks at the bottles. He crosses back to Laurette's unfinished drink and picks it up, using it to chase down the pills. As he sets the drink back down, he gives it a withering look of condescension. He crosses back to the bar, pours himself a shot of whisky, and drains it at a gulp. He crosses downstage and stands, pressing his temples again. After a moment, Marian enters, wearing a shawl. She looks around and shrugs.

Marian: Well, *I* came back at least.

Charlie: Turning. There's one thing to be grateful for. And that's very nice. Your wrap.

Marian: Thank you. A souvenir of . . . somewhere . . . Bern? Basel? Bregenz?

Charlie: Marian, I've been thinking. Maybe we ought to go and see if we can find them. Laurette and Ted. Just see that they're out there somewhere . . . together.

Marian: Certainly. We'll just worry if we stay here.

Charlie: That's right. Worry and drink, probably.

Marian: It's not impossible. I wonder where they'd have gone, though.

Charlie: Does Ted know the town, particularly?

Marian: He seemed to today, but we had maps and guide-books. No, but yesterday . . . he found our way back from the Palace Hotel, certainly better than I would have.

Charlie: Oh yes? And is that an interesting story?

Marian: No.

She smiles.

Charlie: So he might have taken her there? It's certainly a place she'd have been willing to go.

Marian: Well then, we'll make that the focus of our search.

Charlie: And if it's unsuccessful, we can still have a drink.

She glances away as a mild look of puzzlement plays across her face.

Marian: Well, we'll see about that.

They exit.

Scene Three

In the bar at the Lausanne Palace Hotel, Charlie is seated at a small table with drinks. Marian enters.

Charlie: Any luck? Obviously not.

Marian: No, I cased the bar pretty well, and the terrace.

Charlie: We can look again in a bit. Indicating the drinks. I've taken the liberty . . .

Marian: Yes, I see you have.

She sits.

We should probably look in the salon across the way, where the band's playing. There was a bit of a throng in there, so I couldn't really get a good look.

Charlie: Those musicians sound pretty terrific.

Marian: They are, actually. I wouldn't have expected a Swiss jazz band to generate so much heat, but they really do.

Charlie: You heard them then. Last night, probably?

Marian: Yes. Does your wife like to dance, Charlie?

Charlie: You'd think she might, but I've tried to take her places and she won't go. Says she's lost her taste for it.

Marian: Well, I guess that can happen.

Charlie: And Ted? Is he a fiend on the floor?

Marian: I can't . . . say, really. As you know, we only just met.

Charlie: But –

Marian: Yes?

Charlie: Nothing. I don't really care about Ted. I don't know why I'm asking about him.

Marian: Because he's a stranger who's at large with your wife?

Charlie: Oh. Right. *Laughing.* That.

He raises his glass.

Cheers. To Stranger Ted.

Marian lifts her glass thoughtfully and sips.

Alright, listen. I don't think there's cause for worry. You and I have spent the same amount of time together as they have, and I don't consider us to be strangers at this point.

Marian: Really? I'm not sure I agree.

Charlie: Do you think I'm concealing something?

Marian: Probably not. So tell me where you're from, Charlie. Tell me where you live and what you do.

Charlie: Certainly, though I'll apologize in advance for it not being terribly interesting. I'm from Pennsylvania. Allentown, specifically. My family's business was manufacturing. Car parts.

Marian: But you don't still do that?

Charlie: I sold my interest in it. I wanted to come to Europe. I was here during the war, and wanted to see it in different circumstances.

Marian: Oh, so you fought in . . .

Charlie: In France.

Marian: I see. That's where my husband was stationed.

Charlie: And?

Marian: He died, Charlie. And that's not what we're talking about.

Charlie: Still, I'm sorry.

Marian: Thank you. So now you live . . .

Charlie: In Geneva, mostly.

Marian: You've an apartment?

Charlie: No. Hotels are just fine for the present.

Marian: Interesting. No fixed address. Your wife is fine with that?

Charlie: I think she's expressed her fondness for hotel life pretty clearly.

Marian: True enough. And where's she from? Pennsylvania too?

Charlie: No. Virginia, I think. East? West? One of them? We met here. In Switzerland, I mean. Not Lausanne.

Marian: Well well. That's all fairly romantic, I guess. A big adventure, filled with surprises.

Charlie: You say that like it's a criticism.

Marian: Yours just doesn't sound like the sort of life I'm used to, Charlie. One craves the exotic from a distance and then finds it a little unnerving at close range.

Charlie: Now, a conclusion like that must have an interesting story behind it.

Marian: I just don't think I could live in hotels. That's all. I'd need a regular apartment, especially if – . . .

Charlie: Yes?

Marian: No, I won't say that.

Charlie: Oh, come on. I'm not easily upset. You may have noticed that.

Marian: Alright, yes. And it's rude to leave a statement dangling that way. A loathsome conversational gambit. What I was thinking was that . . . I'd need to have a regular apartment, if I was married to someone like your wife. I'm sorry if that's rude.

Charlie: I don't think it is. I understand completely. You'd need stability to be able to handle her . . . instability.

Marian: Yes.

Charlie: Well, maybe you're right. Maybe that's why things aren't so good for us. I should know better. I should have known. I knew perfectly well early on that she was . . . crazy.

Marian: Is that maybe a little harsh?

Charlie: I don't think it is. The thing you have know Marian, that explains a lot of this is that . . . I met Laurette in an insane asylum.

Marian: I beg your pardon?

Charlie: Alright, maybe a mental hospital is closer to what it was, but still, she was a patient there.

Marian: I see. You'll forgive my next question I hope, but –

Charlie: What was I doing there? Marian, I was briefly suffering an affliction myself. A cough. I have some sensitivities from . . . my previous visit to Europe. So I was touring sanatoriums and due to some misinformation ended up at the one where Laurette was . . . resting. Obviously, I realized my error, but not before I was struck by her beauty. And her . . .

Marian: Vivacity?

Charlie: She was just so charming.

Marian: And you just stole her away?

Charlie: She was released. In time. Pause. Are there any more questions?

Marian: No. No, there aren't. I think we should maybe head home. Clearly Laurette and Ted aren't here and they may well be back on the Princess' terrace wondering what on earth has become of us.

Charlie: Sure, we can go, if you like. Checking his pockets. Oh now, we left so suddenly, I didn't think to bring my billfold.

Marian: It's fine. Taking money from her purse. I'll treat.

Charlie: You're kind, madame. I can't buy you a drink here, but I'll certainly pour you another at home.

Marian: That may not be necessary.

Charlie: Oh?

Marian: Standing. I may have had enough. To drink.

Charlie: Standing. Maybe we should have a gander at the dance floor before we go. In case Ted's convinced her to shake a merry leg.

Marian: If he has, then I'm not sure that's something I care to – . . .

Charlie: Yes? Pause. I think you nearly said something quite candid.

Marian: Perhaps. Won't happen again.

They exit.

Scene Four

Back on the terrace of the Maison de la Princesse. Dorrie is gathering up glasses and bottles. Marian and Charlie enter.

Dorrie: Oh, good evening. Mrs. Ogilvy. Mr. Hastings.

Charlie: Princess.

Marian: We went for a little walk. We probably should have said something.

Dorrie: It's fine. You don't have to report your every move.

Marian: I don't suppose Ted and Laurette have come back.

Dorrie: No, they haven't.

Charlie: They didn't sneak upstairs?

Dorrie: There's just the one entrance. I'd have noticed.

Charlie: I hope you're not putting all those bottles away.

Dorrie: Well, I thought everyone was done. I can't leave them out all night.

Charlie: No no, of course not. But be a darling and leave 'em a bit longer. We can bring them inside.

Dorrie: I suppose that'd be alright.

Marian: I'll make sure it happens, Dorrie.

Charlie: I appreciate it, Princess. My wife left me, probably, so a nightcap's in order.

He pours himself a glass of whisky.

Dorrie: To Marian. She left him? You know that now?

Marian: No. Not really. I think we maybe know less than we did before.

Dorrie: How's that?

Marian: Oh, I don't know. I don't know what I mean by that. It's just all rather perplexing.

Dorrie: Well, sit up as long as you like.

Marian: Thanks. I don't know how concerned I should even be about any of this. I'm predicting he won't last much longer, though, drinking at this rate.

Dorrie: Poor man. They were so happy when they checked in. Well good night. Good night, Mr. Hastings.

Charlie: G'night, Princess.

Dorrie exits. Charlie approaches Marian and hands her a glass of Lillet.

Here's one for you. Surprise.

Marian: Oh, I don't know that I –

Charlie: Drink it or don't. I said I'd pour you one, and so I have. Let's sit.

He sits, a little heavily. She sits across from him.

I saw her majesty eyeing me pathetically there before she left. Not sure how much I like that.

Marian: She's a good hostess. She's concerned about the welfare and happiness of her guests.

Charlie: You've got an answer for everything, don't ya?

Marian: I –

Charlie: No no, I think it's terrific. Things don't bog down . . . with you.

Marian: Thanks.

Charlie: We should have asked at the front desk of the Palace, that's what we should have done. They might have just gone right there and checked in. That'd be about the speed she likes to do things.

Marian: Charlie, I really don't think that –

Charlie: That the young Doctor would have been so easily ensnared? He's not one to take up with a gal on a moment's notice? Not one to be swayed by a beautiful unknown lady in a first-class hotel a million miles from home?

Marian: Please, just stop.

Charlie: I'm not saying it's a bad thing, Marian. I'm saying I understand completely. You can say what you like about him, but I think you know I'm right. And I fell into that same trap. I did. And I think you fell into one just like it.

Abruptly he sets down his drink and presses his hands against his forehead.

Ohhhhh . . .

Marian: What is it? What . . .

Charlie: Oh, I just can't get rid of this . . .

Marian: It's your head? You have a headache?

Charlie: It happens. I get these . . . I just need to . . .

He takes out his pill bottle and pops a few pills into his mouth, then washes them down with a gulp of whisky.

Marian: Is that wise? To mix those things?

Charlie: No, strictly speaking, I don't think it is. There's no wisdom in it.

Jeff Haslam as Charlie Hastings, Barbara Gates Wilson as Marian Ogilvy in *The Oculist's Holiday*

Marian: You should just go to bed, Charlie.

Charlie: I will. I will. This just needs to subside a little before I get up. Just . . . just sit there and smile for a bit. I think that'll help.

She sits and looks on. He breathes slowly and deliberately with his head lowered.

There now . . . Not better yet, but not worse . . .

Marian: That's good.

Charlie: Oh, Marian . . .

He reaches across and takes her hands.

Marian: Now . . . Charlie . . . please . . .

Charlie: Not looking up at her. I just have to say thank you. Thanks for staying with me through this.

Marian: You're welcome.

Charlie: Marian, your hands are so cool. Mine are burning up. Can you please just . . .

He raises her hands and presses them against his forehead.

Ohh . . . that's just so nice . . . so cool . . .

Marian: Yes, you really are quite feverish.

He stands abruptly and pulls her up too.

Charlie: Marian, we just need to forget them. We can just do that so easily. It would make things so much better . . . if we could just forget . . .

Marian: That you're married?

Charlie: Oh, I'm not. That was just for appearances, and really unnecessary in this company, as it turns out. Marian . . .

He pulls her toward him rather roughly and attempts to kiss her. She pulls back, but he retains a tight grip on her arms.

Marian: No. No, Charlie! We're not going to do that.

Charlie: Oh come on . . . We'll just have a little fun. Make ourselves feel as good as we can. Might be better than last night, even.

Marian: Alright, that's enough. Let go of my arms.

Charlie: I can't. I don't want to.

Marian: Please let go of my arms. I won't ask you again.

Charlie: Good. I'm tired of that.

They struggle. She gets one arm free, but he retains a grip on the other and they careen around a little, knocking over chairs.

Marian: Oh no, please . . . help . . . Help!

Charlie: Sh sh sh . . .

They struggle a little more, getting a little louder. Dorrie appears at the door.

Dorrie: What the . . . Mr. Hastings! Stop! Stop this!

Charlie: Oh, mind your own business.

Dorrie: That's what I do, pal!

She advances, raising a small revolver, which she places against the side of his head.

Charlie: What's that . . . what . . .

Dorrie: What does it feel like?

Charlie: You've pulled a gun on me? What kind of place is this? We're just having some laughs. Drunk American laughs, Princess. Tell her, Marian . . .

Marian crosses quickly away from Charlie and stands quivering a little, unable to speak.

Alright, now what?

Dorrie: Sit down, Mr. Hastings.

Charlie: Sure. Yes. Happy to do that.

He sits. She continues to point the gun at him.

Dorrie: In a moment, it'll be time to go to your room, Mr. Hastings.

Charlie: Good. I want that. I was wrong to think otherwise.

Dorrie: But before you turn in . . . one last nightcap.

Charlie: I . . . really?

Marian: Dorrie?

Dorrie: We just want things to be normal again, don't we?

Charlie: Oh . . . yes!

Dorrie: Alright then.

She picks up a bottle and pours some in a glass.

Charlie: I was having whisky, actually.

Dorrie: This is better. *Spécialité de la maison.*

Charlie: Fine. Good. It's all appreciated.

Dorrie: Here you are. All in one go. That's the Russian way.

Charlie: You bet.

He drains it at a gulp.

Dorrie: Good. Now good night.

She looks at him expectantly.

Charlie: Oh . . . yes . . .

He gets up a little unsteadily.

G'night, Marian. I hope you'll forgive an' . . . like she's done . . .

He goes toward the exit, turns back with a look of profound bewilderment, then turns and exits. Moments later there is a crash and a clatter from offstage.

Dorrie: Well, that's that. He'll be out for a good twelve hours.

Marian: Dorrie . . . what have you done?

Dorrie: Holding up the bottle she poured from. The Prince had a very strong constitution when it came to drink. I've yet to see him bested.

She sets the bottle aside and approaches Marian.

Poor Marian, are you alright?

Marian: Oh, I have no idea. Embracing Dorrie. Thank you though.

Dorrie: Of course. Now you should go to your room. I'll have the police come take him away.

Marian: Yes, thank you.

She takes a few steps then stops.

I don't want to see him.

Dorrie: No no, of course you don't.

She exits. Marian slumps into a chair and stares ahead.

Scene Five

The following morning, Dorrie is putting away bottles. Marian enters.

Dorrie: Oh, good morning, Mrs. Ogilvy.

Marian: Good morning, Dorrie.

Dorrie: Would you like some breakfast?

Marian: Maybe in a little. I just wanted to know –

Dorrie: Oh, they took him alright. Him and his car. I expect he'll wake up in jail with the drunks. They might hold him longer if you want to make any sort of charges.

Marian: I don't. I can't. I don't even know what it was that happened. Pause. And the others . . .

Dorrie: Haven't come back. I checked their rooms. I'm sorry . . .

Marian: Oh no, don't be. It's all just . . .

Dorrie: Doctor Fletcher's suitcase is still here. He'll have to come back for it.

Marian: Well of course, that's true, but . . . Dorrie, I'm leaving in a few hours. On the train. I can't stay another night.

Dorrie: That's fine. If that's what you want, I quite understand.

Marian: Your house is just lovely, and you've been so kind, but I just can't bear what's happened to me, and I don't only mean last night with that awful Mr. Hastings. I've had two very strange experiences here, and for all that the latter one was so utterly unpleasant, the thing that's thrown me right off balance is how similar the events of both evenings really were. The same forces at play, the same motives. The same opportunities lunged at . . . And now . . . I think back on the last two days and nights and I don't recognize myself in any of it. So I have to leave. I have to leave this afternoon and try to get back to being the woman I was two days ago.

Dorrie: *Crossing and clasping her hands.* Mrs. Ogilvy . . . Marian, I completely understand. Doctor Fletcher may well be disappointed, but –

Marian: But he might also be completely delighted.

Dorrie: You really believe that?

Marian: I don't know what to think. I just need it not to matter to me at all. If he gets back before I leave, I suppose I'll have to see him, but otherwise . . . You can tell him . . . Tell him whatever you like.

She exits.

Scene Six

On a platform in the Lausanne train station. Marian enters with luggage. She stops and sets it down and looks at her ticket. She peers upward for directions, then looks at her watch and picks up the suitcases. As she does this, Ted enters behind her, hurriedly. He looks startled and stops in his tracks.

Ted: Marian?

Marian: *Turning.* Oh no. No, Ted, no . . .

Ted: You're leaving?

Marian: I have to, Ted. My train's in a couple of minutes. Less –

Ted: But –

Marian: Did Dorrie tell you – . . . No . . .

Ted: I just got off a train myself and . . . I'm so sorry, Marian, I –

Marian: Please, Ted, no. You don't have to be. None of this really happened, alright? That's the way it has to be. I'm going.

Ted: No –

Marian: You're very nice, Ted. You're a very nice, likeable young man, but you're still a stranger to me, and that wouldn't be any different if I stayed another day.

Ted: Marian –

Marian: No. My mind is made up, and now we're on the verge of making a scene and that's just more unpleasantness of the sort I really need to be done with, so I really have to go. Good-bye, Ted.

She turns to go.

Ted: Marian, no, I –

He grabs hold of her arm.

Marian: Let go of my arm. Let go of my arm!

He lets go and steps away in alarm. She turns back, takes a breath and speaks calmly.

My train leaves in two minutes. It really does.

She turns and exits. He watches her, backs up a little, then turns and runs off in the opposite direction as train sounds are heard.

Scene Seven

Marian stands centre, tightly lit as in the prologue.

Marian: So there you have it, ladies, the unfortunate conclusion of my European adventure in the spring of 1931. And why do I consider it important for you to know about all that happened to me over those two days and nights? Well, it's just this: If you're to lead happy and productive lives in the coming years, it will be absolutely essential . . . I'll say that word a second time . . . essential . . . for you to be able to distinguish between something that is a genuine threat to your well-being and something which you simply fear because you don't understand it as well as you want to. Pause. I may have left Europe as scheduled at the end of my vacation, but I'm afraid that, like Dr. Wilmer Jarvis of Indiana, I have never actually come home. And I need to tell you, being on an oculist's holiday sounds like it could be a source of infinite pleasure, but it really isn't. Not for me.

Now, I'd like to be able to chat further with you over tea and date squares at the impending reception, and maybe even talk about a few of the subjects I was expected to address when I was invited here. But instead, I'm going to have to wish you all the very best of luck with your careers and be on my way. You see . . . I have a boat to catch.

She flees.

Scene Eight

At the Maison de la Princesse, Dorrie sits on the terrace, reading a book. Marian enters, a little cautiously.

Marian: Excuse me . . . Princess . . .

Dorrie: Looking up. Oh . . . hello . . . I'm sorry. I wasn't expecting . . . oh?

Marian: Hello Dorrie.

Dorrie: It's you . . . Mrs . . .

Marian: Ogilvy. Marian. I'm glad to find you still here.

Dorrie: You're on another holiday? Are you wanting to check in? Because I do have –

Marian: No no. I'm up at the Palace Hotel. It's just . . . simpler.

Dorrie: Yes, of course.

Marian: I mean . . . free of certain associations. The Palace is pretty much free of any other simplicities, which is a good thing, given what they're charging. Pause. May I sit for a little?

Dorrie: Of course . . . please. Would you like some coffee?

Marian: Oh, yes . . . I really think I would.

Dorrie: Good.

She retrieves a cup and pours some coffee from a pot.

Marian: I'm so glad to see you, Dorrie. I already said that, but I'm saying it again because it's just so true. I worried I might come here and find, I don't know . . . nothing. Someone else.

Dorrie: You think I'd leave this place?

Marian: Well, you do have your adventurous life . . .

Dorrie: Not in the way I once did. Which is fine.

Marian: Well, good. It's good to . . . know where one belongs . . .

Dorrie looks at her quizzically.

I'm a little nervous, Dorrie. Can you tell?

Dorrie: I think there are some things you'd like to ask me.

Marian: Yes, of course. But it feels presumptuous in a way to assume that you're going to remember details about my stay here after three years have –

Dorrie: Not many unpleasant things have happened in my house, Marian. So I recall it all pretty well.

Marian: Alright, yes. I think maybe it won't be a surprise if the first question I ask is about Doctor Fletcher. Did he come back here?

Dorrie: Yes, he did. The afternoon of the day you left. He told me he'd seen you at the station, but that your train was leaving and you'd barely had time to talk.

Marian: That's how he put it?

Dorrie: Yes. I imagined something a little more complicated might have taken place. I knew you could have taken a later train if you'd wanted to.

Marian: Yes.

Dorrie: And I told him right away what had happened with you and Charlie Hastings. He was horrified and I think if you were brusque with Ted, he may well have understood.

Marian: Well . . . thank you for that.

Dorrie: And then he told me what had happened with himself and that woman. Laurette.

Marian looks at Dorrie expectantly.

Scene Nine

Lights cross-fade and Laurette is discovered walking furiously on a street.

Ted: Offstage. Laurette! Laurette, wait!

Laurette: No, leave me alone. I said I didn't want to see you anymore.

Ted: Entering. It's not Charlie, Laurette. It's me, Ted.

Laurette: Stopping. Oh, it figures they'd send the doctor.

Ted: Laurette, that's not fair. We're just worried about you, out here alone.

Laurette: Oh come on, it's Switzerland. What can happen to me?

Ted: Well, maybe nothing, but . . . I understand your desire to just walk away like you did, but walking away even a short distance isn't always a good idea when you don't quite know where you are.

Laurette: Alright, sure. I was just so angry.

Ted: So I've been around the area a bit and I can tell you maybe . . . if you want to go sit on a park bench for a bit, then you should go that way, or if you want to go walk by the lake, it's straight down there, and if you want to go to a little café, there are two nice-looking ones right around the corner here. I'm not going to try to drag you back inside, Laurette.

Laurette: Good. Thank you, Ted. You're a gentleman. I'm sorry if I implied you weren't.

Ted: I don't think you did, really. So, do you know where you might like to go? You can take a moment to think.

Laurette: I don't have to. The train station.

Ted: Really?

Laurette: Oh, I'd say so. There's nothing to keep me here. I'm done with Charlie.

Ted: You're leaving him? Your marriage is –

Laurette: Oh, it's not real. We were just lying about that, so we'd get treated better at hotels. It was fun to pretend, but I'm so glad to be done with it now. Charlie's a charmer and all, but between you and me, I'm pretty sure he's not so rich as he makes himself out to be. He said little hotels were better on account of their being more discreet, but what the hell does that matter when you're saying you're married? Sorry to use that sort of language, but it's just frustrating. He thinks I'm not the type that notices things, but I can tell when I've been sold a bill of goods.

Ted: So . . . where would you be off to . . . on the train?

Laurette: Well, Geneva, I guess, if that's near here. It can't be that far if it's on the same lake.

Ted: It'd be about an hour's trip.

Laurette: Oh, that's nothing. That's just fine. And I have friends there. Lots of friends I can call. So can you show me the way? To the station?

Ted: I can certainly do that. I'll just go back in and tell –

Laurette: No! Charlie can't know. He can't know I've left till I'm gone. You know what I mean.

Ted: But . . . I should . . . tell . . .

Laurette: Who? The others? The widow lady? How are you going to do that without Charlie finding –

Ted: Yes, you're right. And it really isn't going to take long at all. It's not far, if you don't mind taking the short, steep route.

Laurette: Anything. I'd climb anything to get away from him.

Ted: You do realize that eventually I'm going to have to be the one to go back and break the news to him. That might be unpleasant.

Laurette: Sure, but you're a doctor. You've got loads of experience with that, don't ya?

Ted: Sadly, no. I've never lost a patient.

Laurette: Well, I guess there's a first for everything. *Taking his arm.* Come on now, Doctor Ted, lead the way.

Light fades as they walk off. Light comes up in another area, where Laurette stands alone, looking mildly agitated. Ted enters with a train ticket and schedules.

Ted: Alright, I have your ticket here. The train's in about fifteen minutes.

Laurette: Thanks, Ted. Sorry about the money. I wish I had some, but –

Ted: I know, it's all unexpected. And it's not expensive.

Laurette: I'd like to pay you back if –

Ted: Don't even think about it.

Laurette: Right. You just want me out of your life.

Ted: I liked it better when you said I was a gentleman.

Laurette: Oh yes. And you still are.

Ted: So . . . the train'll be leaving from platform three, which is right over there. It'll probably be pulling in in about five minutes.

Laurette: Alright. So just . . . right there?

Ted: Do you want me to wait with you, or –

Laurette: No, you want to get back, don't you?

Ted: I really should.

Laurette: So go. I'll just wait and . . . Looking at the ticket. Are there other stops before Geneva?

Ted: A few, I think. Looking at the ticket. Just three. Quick ones.

Laurette: Three. That's not many. Alright. Run along then. Thanks for everything.

Ted: Alright. Good-bye, Laurette. Good luck. Safe journey.

Laurette: Thanks.

He exits. She stands and looks at her ticket absently, then looks around, with a vaguely troubled expression. She begins to look a little anxious, and begins breathing rather quickly, but brings this under control. A train is heard approaching and as it does, she again begins hyperventilating and emitting sharp little cries of panic, which escalate into full-blown screams.

Laurette: Ted! Ted!! Oh God, Ted, I can't, I can't, I can't . . . Tedddddd!!!

Ted re-enters hurriedly and runs to her.

Ted: Laurette, Laurette, what's wrong?

Laurette: Clutching him. I can't do it, Ted. I can't take the train by myself. I'm afraid!

Ted: Alright now, alright. You don't have to. Just try to let yourself breathe . . . Just hold onto me, not too tight because then you can't relax, and that's what you need to do so you can . . .

Laurette: Yes yes . . . I know . . . I know how to do it . . .

She slows her breathing carefully and as she does so, she slides down so she's sitting flat on the floor.

Ted: Laurette, maybe . . .

Laurette: I need to sit right down, here. That makes it . . . better . . . I should have just . . . done that . . .

She breathes carefully. He kneels beside her.

Ted: Laurette . . . do you need me to go with you on the train? To Geneva? I can do that if it'll help you.

Laurette: Yes . . . yes . . . I think . . . Ted . . . ?

Ted: What, yes, I'm here.

Laurette: Ted, I need to tell you something . . .

Ted: Alright, go ahead.

Laurette: I don't . . . know anyone in Geneva. I shouldn't go there. I've been to some parties probably but . . . I don't have anybody I can . . .

Ted: Well then . . . is there somewhere else . . .

Laurette: Yes. Please don't be angry.

Ted: I'm not. I won't be.

Mat Busby as Ted Fletcher, Davina Stewart as Laurette Hastings in *The Oculist's Holiday*

Laurette: In the town of Avenches . . . I live . . . in a sort of a clinic, with a residence . . . It's like a hospital and I have to stay there because of . . . how I get . . . how I was just now . . .

Ted: And that's where you were living before you went driving with Charlie?

Laurette: Yes. I'm not supposed to leave. My husband pays for me to stay there. My second husband. Back home. He's nice, but we couldn't stay married, you see, because . . . Anyway, I'm not supposed to leave there but the grounds aren't completely walled in. There's a stream you can just cross and –

Ted: Charlie made you leave? He stole you out of there?

Laurette: No. He convinced me. I allowed that. I wasn't stolen. I'm not . . . helpless . . . I didn't think I was . . . helpless . . .

Ted: So what was he doing there?

Laurette: Having treatments . . . of some sort. Not like me . . . He could come and go. We met on the grounds. He'd always visit . . . It was nice . . . Now it's just awful . . . I need to go back.

Ted: Alright, Laurette, of course you do. Let me see this schedule.

He takes the ticket and schedule from her and looks at it.

So . . . Avenches . . . that's about an hour and a half in the other direction. And there's a train in about forty-five minutes.

Laurette: Oh, thank heaven . . . Will you –

Ted: Of course, Laurette. I'll go with you. I'll take you there. Just promise me . . . Just tell me that this is the truth, finally. This is where you really need to go?

Laurette: It is, Ted. Looking him in the eyes. I was lying to you before, but I'm not lying now.

Ted: Good. Good. I believe you.

Laurette: Oh Ted, you're so kind.

Ted: Oh I don't know. I just want to fix things when they're wrong. If that's kindness, well . . . Helping her up. Now . . . we need to trade in that ticket and get another for me. And I think you'd better come along to the wicket this time.

Laurette: Yes. No argument here.

They exit. Train sounds are heard. After a moment they walk into another light.

Ted: Alright, this looks like it. It's through the gate there?

Laurette: Yes. I'll have to ring for admittance. So this is where you leave me.

Ted: I don't have to. I want to see that you get in alright.

Laurette: No, Ted. I don't you to be there. You could get in trouble.

Ted: Why? I haven't done anyth –

Laurette: They won't believe that. They'll just ask you so many questions, and if you have no answers . . . It's simpler this way. I left. I came back. I'll say what I remember and maybe it'll all be over quickly. You should go now. You'll want to get back to . . . ahhh . . . where were we?

Ted: Lausanne.

Laurette: Yes, right.

Ted: *Taking out a little pad and scribbling.* It's late now. I'm not even sure I'll be able to get a train back until morning.

Laurette: Oh, poor Ted.

Ted: I'm sure it'll all work out. And maybe Charlie will have left by now and we won't have to have that confrontation.

Laurette: That'd be good at least. What are you writing?

Ted: It's just the places you were and the train you arrived on. If they demand that information, you'll have it now.

He folds the paper and puts in securely in her hand.

There you go.

Laurette: Thank you. *Putting it a pocket.* That's very thoughtful.

Ted: Don't lose that. Make sure you –

Laurette: Oh don't worry, they'll get it. I'm about to be very thoroughly searched. I should go now, while I've still got the nerve.

Ted: I'll wait till you ring the bell?

Laurette: Yes, please, but stay back here.

Ted: Yes.

Laurette: Alright. *Pause. She clasps his hands.* Thank you, Ted.

Ted: You're welcome, Laurette.

Laurette: Here we go.

She turns and exits. He waits. A bell rings. He watches for a few more seconds, then waves, nods, and exits quickly.

Scene Ten

Marian and Dorrie are on the terrace, as before.

Dorrie: And he was right. It was late morning before he was finally able to get a train back here.

Marian: Then he'd just gotten off it when we met at the station. When I dismissed him from my life. Tried to . . .

She turns to Dorrie.

I was an idiot, Dorrie.

Dorrie: You couldn't have known.

Marian: But I acted as though I did. As though I knew . . . something. And I didn't know anything at all. And you haven't . . . seen him again?

Dorrie: No. He stayed one more night and then left before breakfast. We didn't speak of anything else.

Marian: I have to find him, Dorrie. How am I going to do that?

Dorrie: Well, I know where you can find Laurette. She may know something.

Marian: Will they let me see her? In that place?

Dorrie: Oh, she's not there. She's here in Lausanne, and she's quite changed. I saw her one day, and nearly didn't recognize her.

Marian: Well, where –

Dorrie: Conveniently, she seems to be working at the Palace Hotel. I see her coming and going from the service entrance.

Marian: Oh?

Dorrie: Yes, so that's easy. I should tell you that Charlie Hastings is still at large here as well. I don't know that he's ever left town. He's very changed too, only not for the better. You'd hardly know it was him, and he certainly wouldn't know you.

Marian: Something's happened to him? Obviously.

Dorrie: I think he's very sick. He probably always was. Now he just wanders outdoors.

Marian: Is he living on the street? Is that even allowed here?

Dorrie: There are some unfortunates who spend their days in the parks and so forth. Then some of our hardier Franciscans round them up and take them into the church at night. I think that's Mr. Hastings' life now.

Marian: I . . . well, I don't know what to say about that.

Dorrie: Don't say anything. Just go to your hotel.

Marian: Yes. Thank you, Dorrie.

She exits as lights fade.

Scene Eleven

At the hotel. Laurette sits at a small desk, looking at a lined notebook with jottings in it. Her hair is primly put up and she's wearing glasses and a beautician's smock. She looks up as Marian enters.

Laurette: Madame.

Marian: Good afternoon . . . Laurette?

Laurette: Yes, that's me. You must be Mrs. Carmichael.

Marian: Oh no, I'm not.

Laurette: Oh . . . I thought that's who was next on the . . . *Looking at the schedule.* Yes, I was right. I'm sorry, maybe you've just come to make an appointment. For your hair? Nails?

Marian: No, actually . . . I just wanted to talk to *you* about something, Laurette. If you're expecting a client, though, I can certainly come back.

Laurette: Well she's not really due for another ten minutes, so it should be fine. What's this about? Do I know you?

Marian: We met once. May I sit?

Laurette: Please.

Marian: *Sitting across from her.* My name is Marian Ogilvy. We met a few years back, here in Lausanne at the Maison de la Princesse.

Laurette: Oh! That place I went with –

Marian: With Charlie Hastings, that's right. I was one of the people you met at that little party.

Laurette: The one I stormed away from. Yes. Oh, I'm embarrassed. I'm sorry I didn't recognize you, but –

Marian: No, that's fine, I really didn't expect you to.

Laurette: *Gasping.* But then . . . you know Ted! Don't you? Doctor Fletcher? You must! You can tell me how I might find him.

Marian: *After a pause.* No. I can't. I was actually hoping you might know that.

Laurette: Oh, how I wish I did, Mrs. Ogilvy. Doctor Fletcher saved my life. I'd certainly have gone right out my mind if it weren't for him.

Marian: What happened, Laurette? What did he do? Actually I do know that he took you back to Avenches, to that clinic. But you saw him again?

Laurette: No, I never did, but you see . . . When he left me there, he gave me a note that was supposed to say where all I'd been, but what it really said was that I should be examined immediately for a severe astigmatism, and I would probably need eye surgery and to wear spectacles for the rest of my life. And he was right. I was . . . not blind exactly, but my vision was just so crazy . . . things coming in and out of focus . . . no sense of distance, and it was just what I was used to so I never thought . . . It was why I would get so frightened sometimes, and then so angry when I didn't understand what was going on around me. It was why I seemed to be . . . ill.

Marian: And you'd had never had your eyes looked at before?

Laurette: No, I hadn't. I just never thought I was the sort of person who wore glasses. I was . . . foolish. And vain. And in Avenches, they were only interested in giving me pills and asking me questions about my thoughts and my dreams. I was glad to be done with all that.

Marian: And Charlie . . . He was a patient there too?

Laurette: Never really officially. I found out a little about him before I left. He had something they couldn't really do anything about . . . from the war. Some condition that was going to deteriorate over time.

Marian: It was . . . in his lungs?

Laurette: No. Not if he was in that place. Pause. They'd have kept him there happily enough, but he didn't really have any money. He'd been well-to-do, but lost a lot with everyone else in '29. I think the day he took off with me was when they'd told him he couldn't come back.

Marian: He's still around, apparently. In Lausanne.

Laurette: I know he is. I've passed him in the street a couple of times, and seen him in the park. I half think I should say something to him, but then I get afraid. Pause. I feel like I should thank him. Is that silly? Strange?

Marian: I don't think it is, Laurette. If he hadn't done what he did –

Laurette: Exactly. And of course who I'd really like to thank is Doctor Fletcher, but he must be long gone from these parts. I expect he's gone back home to America.

Marian: You know . . . I have a hunch he might not have done that.

Laurette: Really? Well, if you can find him, please tell him how I turned out. Tell him how happy I am and that I can read. I can read train schedules and signs and books. I read and read, and when I'm not at work I'll go for big long stretches where I don't talk at all. I used to say such stupid things, Mrs. Ogilvy. I just couldn't help it.

Marian: You mustn't be hard on yourself for that. And I do hope I can find Ted and tell him all those things. I only wonder now where to start . . . Laurette, this may sound silly, but if you were to set up practice as an optometrist in Switzerland, but didn't really speak French very well at all, where would you do that?

Laurette: Well . . . I think . . . in Montreux. That's where all the Americans like to go now, so –

Marian: Montreux? That's near here, yes?

Laurette: It is. It's just along the lake, at the far end. It's not a very long train ride at all.

Marian clasps Laurette's hand and squeezes it tightly.

Marian: Oh, but it's probably going to feel like one.

Scene Twelve

In an optometrist's office, Marian sits in a chair, wearing a dark veil. Ted enters wearing a white lab coat over his suit, and carrying a clipboard with charts.

Ted: Good afternoon. You'd be Mrs. Carmichael, our surprise last patient?

Marian: In slightly lowered voice. Yes, doctor. Thank you for seeing me on such short notice.

Ted: It's no trouble, Mrs. Carmichael. People aren't usually in a big rush to get in here, so I was rather intrigued when they told me how eager you were to make an appointment. Something's wrong? With your eyes?

Marian: Maybe. The thing is . . . I haven't been able to see things clearly for a very long time, and suddenly so much has been revealed that I'm worried.

He looks at her, intently.

Ted: Worried . . . how?

Marian: My senses are all overwhelmed. Right now . . . I can scarcely bring myself to speak.

He smiles a little.

Ted: Well, you don't need to, Mrs. Carmichael. You don't need to say a thing. But . . . would you mind standing up?

Marian: Oh . . . alright . . .

He takes her hand and helps her up. He looks at her thoughtfully, still smiling a little.

Oh . . . I'm a little giddy. I don't know if –

Ted: I think it's to be expected. Still holding her hand. I've got you. And now . . . you're going to have to show me your eyes.

Marian: Yes . . . yes . . . but I'm a little embarrassed. You may find them to be rather filled with tears.

Ted: That's fine. Then you won't need drops.

Slowly she pulls off the veil and they stare at one another.

I must say . . . I don't think you have anything to worry about. Your eyes look just fine.

Marian: You know . . . yours do too. Ted.

Ted: Marian . . .

They move in close. He hesitates.

Who's Mrs. Carmichael?

Marian: No one. No one at all.

They kiss as the lights fade.

Scene Thirteen

In a park. Laurette sits on a bench. She has a small paper bag in her lap. After a moment, Charlie enters. His clothes are worn, his appearance is generally rough and somewhat bleary-eyed, and his hands dart and shake a little, involuntarily. He looks at Laurette and the bench, nods a little, and starts to cross.

Laurette: It's alright . . . sir. You can sit here. I don't mind.

Charlie: *Stopping.* Ahhh . . . an American . . .

Laurette: Yes. Like you . . . perhaps?

Charlie: Oh . . . once . . .

He shuffles over and sits on the other end of the bench.

Thanks for . . . *Pointing at the bench* . . . this. The next one's . . . so far . . .

Laurette: Of course. And the view's probably nicer here.

Charlie: Yeah. It's . . . great . . .

They sit in silence for a moment.

Laurette: You know . . . I have a sandwich here that I'm not going to eat. I thought I'd be hungry, but I'm just not. Maybe you'd like it?

Charlie: Really . . . you . . . want . . .

Laurette: Please, yes, take it. I think you deserve it.

Charlie: I may . . . who knows?

She hands him the bag. He sets it on his lap.

Thank you.

Laurette: And thank you.

Charlie: For . . . taking it?

Laurette: Sure.

There is another little pause. He turns to her.

Charlie: Don't . . . watch me eat.

Laurette: No, of course. I won't. I'll be on my way now.

Charlie: Thank you . . . again.

Laurette: You're welcome.

Charlie: And . . . have . . . a good holiday.

Laurette: Oh, I'm not on one. I live here. I work here.

Charlie: Oh . . . not like me . . . My holiday . . . goes on and on . . .

Laurette: Like this great big lake?

Charlie: Yes . . .

They look off for a moment.

Laurette: Well . . . good-bye.

He nods and smiles a little. She exits.

Charlie: After a little. On and on . . . it goes . . . on and on . . .

He holds the bag close and continues to sit, squinting his eyes approvingly at the day.

Slow fade.

WITNESS TO A CONGA

Andrew MacDonald-Smith as Martin, Briana Buckmaster as Laura in *Witness to a Conga* (photo by Jeff Haslam)

PRODUCTION HISTORY

Witness to a Conga was first performed by Teatro La Quindicina in August of 2010, at the Varscona Theatre in Edmonton. It was part of the Edmonton International Fringe Theatre Festival.

CAST

Martin Lowell – Andrew MacDonald-Smith
Laura – Briana Buckmaster
Sheila Waverly – Belinda Cornish
Eleanor Kirk – Sheri Somerville
Walter Lowell – Jeff Haslam
Claire – Leona Brausen

Director – Stewart Lemoine
Costume Designer – Leona Brausen
Lighting Designer – Bobby Smale
Set Designer – Jeff Haslam and Belinda Cornish
Stage Manager – Gina Moe
Assistant Stage Manager – Rachel Rudd

CHARACTERS

Martin Lowell – mid-twenties
Laura – mid-twenties
Sheila Waverly – early thirties
Eleanor Kirk – late forties
Walter Lowell – late forties
Claire – late forties

SETTING

Witness to a Conga is primarily set in Vancouver in the present, with occasional flashbacks and forays to other locations. The times and places are noted by Martin in his narrative and are not suggested through significant visual adjustments, other than costuming in the Venetian scene.

The set for the premiere production consisted of two significant areas on either side of the Varscona stage, diagonally bisected by a snaking path of overlapping mats. The stage right area was dominated by a rather imposing dining room table and chairs, which was the setting for Walter and Eleanor's revelation to Martin of their impending divorce, and also served as a background for Sheila and Martin's teaching scenes, and Eleanor's post-concert trauma scene with Claire. The stage left side held three chairs and a lower coffee table, which was used for various locations, including Martin and Laura's opening scene, Sheila's office, Claire's living room, and the coffee shop in New York. Briefer transitional scenes took place on the path, and Martin's solo narrative moments were generally downstage in a tight spotlight.

MUSIC

The music underscoring Martin's various painful or awkward memories, those involving his parents and Sheila Waverly is all taken from the Overture to Richard Wagner's (1813–1883) early opera *Rienzi*. It's a work of rather deliberate grandeur, largely free of the complex harmonic language Wagner would employ in his later works, and its appropriateness in this instance is tied to Martin's need to artificially ramp up the nobility of certain recollections to make them bearable.

The offstage selection played by Eleanor in the "cookie" scene at Claire's is the "Andante" from Mozart's *Piano Sonata #5,* and the excerpt of Eleanor's playing heard on the radio earlier is the middle movement from Chopin's *Piano Concerto #2.* Both recordings used in our production featured the Portuguese pianist Maria João Pires, as it seemed essential that music supposedly made by Eleanor should be consistently played by a single female performer.

Finally, the work which wraps everything up is the *Conga del Fuego* by the Mexican composer Arturo Márquez. A favorite piece of the Venezuelan conductor Gustavo Dudamel, this work gained prominence through his performances and later recording of it with the Simón Bolívar Youth Orchestra. The use of a conga for full orchestra, rather than say, a nightclub combo or jazz band, is essential here. The arrival of this new music doesn't merely represent Martin "lightening up" for once; rather it's a wholesale reinvention of his life, but one which is made with all prior components still included.

WITNESS TO A CONGA

In the darkness, Latin music of mounting excitement is heard. It cuts out abruptly as Martin is revealed in a tightly lit area.

Martin: I may have seen a conga. I feel like I have. Just not in real life, and certainly not recently. In a movie maybe? In the background, while other people talked at a party. But not close up. And yet, I think I understand what goes on in them. In conga lines. There's a specific foot sequence that's expected. The steps, is what I'd guess they'd be. But probably not everybody observes them. Because it seems to me that congas happen late in the party, when all bets are off. Under controlled competitive ballroom conditions, it'd probably be different. But you don't really see that. You don't see conga competitions on TV, with commentators telling you how everyone in the line is doing and whether the whole is the sum of its parts. Or maybe they do and that's just on a channel I don't watch. There certainly are more than a few of those.

The light expands to reveal Laura. She holds a folder with some documents and a pen.

Laura: Martin?

Martin: What?

Laura: I asked you a question. Are we going to want the band to play a conga at the wedding?

Martin: I heard you. I was just thinking it through.

Laura: And?

Martin: I didn't finish. Maybe just check "yes," so we're covered.

Laura: I don't know if I want to do that. They're just so chaotic, aren't they? Congas. Fun, I guess, but no one will really miss it if it isn't there.

Martin: Then let's say no.

Laura: Alright. *Jots on paper.* No. No to the conga. *Pause.* Now I feel like a killjoy. That's not right when you're planning a wedding.

Martin: Especially your own.

Laura: I want people to enjoy themselves. Just not . . .

Martin: Exuberantly?

Laura: No, you know, I think that'd be fine. I'm going to change this. We can have a conga and people who don't like it can sit it out.

Martin: They'll just watch?

Laura: Or ignore it altogether.

Martin: Can you do that? Ignore a conga?

They look at each other.

Laura: Maybe we shouldn't shouldn't get married.

Martin: Laura?

Laura: A little extreme? I think the decisions are just going to become more and more difficult.

Martin: As we approach the happiest day of our lives. I thought that was sort of the joke.

Laura: Oh, okay. Maybe if I think of it that way . . . In fact . . .

Martin: Yes?

Laura: The more harrowing the wedding gets . . . the more likely it is that the subsequent marriage will seem like a giant relief. I should embrace that notion, though probably without thinking it through.

Martin: No, maybe you're right. We shouldn't have the party.

Laura: You mean the reception?

Martin: Oh no, I meant everything.

Laura: Just walk away? Right now?

Martin: Think of it . . . no conga. At all.

Laura: Till one of us ends up at someone else's wedding and . . .

Martin: I suppose it's unavoidable.

Laura: So we're back on?

Martin: Forever.

Laura: Wonderful.

She leans over and kisses him, then looks at the sheet.

I'm going to leave this issue unresolved for now. The uncertainty of it just makes me feel so alive.

Martin: I get that. But you know . . . we really wouldn't have to be struggling with this if your parents were willing to spring for a full symphony orchestra.

Laura: Because they wouldn't program a conga?

Martin: I figger.

Laura: With the right mix of symphonic selections, everyone could maybe just pass the evening in rapt contemplation and there'd be no dancing whatsoever.

Martin: Truly, we think as one.

Laura: Mmm. Not gonna happen. You'll have to content yourself with the orchestra that's in your head.

Martin: I should never have told you about that. It was a mistake.

Laura: To share a confidence with your future wife?

Martin: No, you're right. That was galvanizing and I enjoyed it. But . . . if we had an orchestra there, the place would be instantly packed with musicians and we wouldn't have to worry about inviting all those other sketchy people.

Laura: Our friends and relations?

Martin: Just for a start.

Laura: You know, I really am going to need you to write out a guest list, sooner rather than later.

Martin: But I don't want to invite anyone to this.

Laura: I'm not sure how to feel about that.

Martin: It's a tribute to how much I enjoy your family and friends.

Laura: Great, but who am *I* gonna talk to?

Martin: Okay, I'll pull something together.

He takes her notepad and pen and jots a little.

What's my limit?

Laura: What, now you think you might have too many?

Martin: I meant my lower limit.

Laura: You know, it's a chance to visit with people you haven't seen in a while. Old friends . . . colleagues . . . the people of your life. Who you like . . .

He looks at her for a bit and smiles.

What?

Martin: I adore your wisdom.

He writes down another name and hands her the pad.

Laura: Looking at it. Three people.

Martin: Six with guests.

Laura: And the first and second ones . . . probably don't care for each other particularly.

Martin: I didn't write my family history. And these are the obvious people, right?

Laura: Sure they are. In fact, they're so obvious that they're already on *my* list. The third one's progress, though. Sheila Waverly. I don't think I know who that it is.

Martin: A university friend. An influential teacher of mine.

Laura: Nice. A dotty professor lady?

Martin: Not exactly. Those aren't allowed in the Comp Lit Department.

Laura: But she isn't an old flame?

Martin: Certainly not.

Laura: Good. Then she can come. I'll need her address.

Martin: Sure. I don't even know if she's still in town.

Laura: Well find out, would ya.

Martin: You want me to lift a finger?

Belinda Cornish as Sheila Waverly in *Witness to a Conga*
(photo by Andrew MacDonald-Smith)

Laura: I know, I know. Careful what you wish for . . .

Light goes out on Laura and she exits. Martin is left in a tight spotlight.

Martin: When you make a list of the people who ought to be present at your wedding, I guess it should go without saying that the great love of your life would be one of them. And the thing about Sheila Waverly is that every time I think about her, the orchestra in my head tells me that that's what she is.

As music plays, Sheila is revealed in a separate light, dressed elegantly and simply, with her hair up. She turns slowly perusing a book, and after a moment begins reading aloud from it. She has a British accent.

Sheila: "Fig-trees surrounded the kitchens; a wood of sycamores stretched away to meet masses of verdure, where the pomegranate shone amid the white tufts of the cotton-plant; vines, laden with grapes, grew up into the branches of the pines; a field of roses bloomed beneath the plane-trees; here and there lilies rocked upon the turf; the paths were strewn with black sand mingled with powdered coral, and in the centre the avenue of cypress formed, as it were, a double colonnade of green obelisks from one extremity to the other."

She looks up.

So it seems that in *Salammbo,* Flaubert has temporarily abandoned the principle of *le mot juste,* and is instead getting paid by the word. Smiling. It's a lesson to us all and the point is simply that everyone's guilty of padding now and then. Just don't do it on the papers you write for me. Three thousand words worth of insight is not a lot when the work in question is *Madame Bovary,* and as the paper I read to you earlier proves, the task I set you is not an impossible one. So that's all for today. Please take your papers from the side table as you go, and I hope you'll enjoy my comments.

With a little wink, she turns to go. Martin approaches.

Martin: Excuse me . . . Professor Waverly . . .

Sheila: Oh . . . yes . . . *Glancing at the paper in her hand.* Martin. You'll be wanting this. *Handing him the essay.* Good work.

Martin: Thank you. It was . . . odd . . . to hear it out loud.

Sheila: Well I thought it was important for the class to know that someone knows what they're doing. And how it should be done.

Martin: Thanks . . . I didn't realize . . .

Sheila: That everyone else was so incompetent? It's always a bit of a shock.

Martin: I'm glad you didn't tell them it was mine.

Sheila: Yes, well, that could have been ugly. And Martin, I think it's important to say, it's not just competence you have. Your assumptions and conclusions are terrific and well-supported.

Martin: So did I break any new ground?

Sheila: I'm going to say no, but you discovered some things about *Madame Bovary* that I once discovered and, like me, I think you did it by paying attention while you were reading.

Martin: I do to try to do that.

Sheila: And I appreciate it.

Martin: Good. Well, thanks again.

He turns to go.

Sheila: Say, Martin . . . have you picked a major?

Martin: Turning back. No, not really.

Sheila: Well I hope you'll give Comp Lit some serious consideration. Too many smarties default to the English Department, and that always strikes me as a shame.

Martin: Oh . . . well . . . Yes, I'll definitely think about that.

He crosses to another light, as hers goes out.

Having an orchestra in your head is both a blessing and a curse, I think. It can make simple things transcendently important and this can in turn make it difficult for you to get on with the business of living. When I'm with Laura, I almost never hear music. We're just too busy talking, and that's probably why marrying her seems like such a good idea. But I'm grateful for the orchestra in other circumstances. Thinking about my parents, for example, is really only bearable with some significant sonic reinforcement.

Music plays, as Eleanor and Walter appear. They come forward holding hands then separate and stand apart. Sheila reappears and the three stand still in separate lights as music thunders forth. Music and light fades and they disappear.

So you've seen the people who haunt me. What's interesting is that only one of them is dead. The other two are really just a phone call away, not that that makes anything easier. In fact I have a lot more conversations with the one who's no longer living. That'd be my mother.

Eleanor appears in a separate light.

Mom, I need you to weigh in on something. Should we have a conga at the wedding?

Eleanor: A conga? You're not serious.

Martin: No, I am. It came up on an official form. A decision has to be made.

Eleanor: A conga? That's like the bunny hop, right?

Martin: I think it maybe is. It's like the bunny hop, but without the hopping.

Eleanor: I think it's a hideous proposition. Don't do it.

Martin: But –

Eleanor: No Martin, I mean it. Why would you want your wedding to disintegrate into that sort of shambles?

Martin: I don't think it necessarily –

Eleanor: Something like that belongs on a playground. It's no way to be marking the union of two grownup people.

Martin: I think Laura is leaning toward –

Eleanor: Well just do what she wants then. She'll be there and I won't, but know this . . . I would definitely opt out of attending a wedding where there was going to be a conga.

Martin: Even mine?

Eleanor: Especially yours.

Martin: Wow. And that's it? There's no arguing with you?

Eleanor: I'd say that's up to you.

Martin: You're right, but I don't care enough about this. Begone phantom!

Eleanor: Oh!

She disappears.

Martin: My mother was Eleanor Kirk, the renowned concert pianist whose career was cut short by crippling arthritis in her hands. This affliction was also more or less directly the cause of her death, though poor judgment was a factor there too. I suppose my propensity for hearing music everywhere has something to do with her influence, though I certainly didn't inherit any of her abilities.

My father is Walter Lowell, the political economist and lecturer. You may have heard of him; a few years ago there was quite a celebrated book that came out examining the fall of the Roman Empire from an entirely Marxist perspective. My father didn't write that. In fact he found its assumptions to be entirely ludicrous, and this was the subject of *his* book. That's his kind of fun.

Light comes up on Claire at a little table, in the midst of potting a plant.

That's Claire. When my mother left my father after fifteen grindingly uncomfortable years of marriage, it was to be with her. *That's* juicy, yeah?

There's a pause. Quiet piano music is heard.

There's music here too. But I think it's just cause she's got the radio on.

He crosses to Claire.

Claire: Looking up. Martin! I was just thinking about you.

He leans in and gives her a little kiss on the cheek.

Martin: Good morning Claire. You were thinking of me . . . in connection with this potting soil?

Claire: Instead of it. Dirt doesn't always hold my attention. I was just wondering how your wedding plans are proceeding.

Martin: I guess they're picking up steam. Decisions are being made. And deferred.

Claire: Well if you need me to do anything . . .

Martin: I'm hoping you'll give me away.

Claire: I don't think that happens with the groom.

Martin: But what if it's what I want? It's not illegal probably.

Claire: No, but . . . If someone were to give you away, it should probably be your father.

Martin: See now, the point I'd be making if you did it is –

Claire: Yeah, I get it. I appreciate it, but . . . Have you actually called him? Pause. You haven't.

Martin: Nag.

Claire: You really have to do it, Martin.

Martin: Scold.

Claire: You're not actually thinking about excluding him, are you?

Martin: No. Not in any sort of active way.

Claire: So you're just putting it off? That's so practical.

Martin: Isn't it. It's because it's so easy to do. Pause. What?

Claire: Nothing. I'm done weighing in on this topic. What should I be thinking about wearing? Is there some official outfit for someone in my position?

Martin: I don't know. I don't think so. A dress . . . that you like.

Claire: I could wear a mannish frock coat. That'd pull a little focus.

Martin: I'd say go for it, but I think it's what I'm wearing.

Claire: Right, and people might compare our figures if we were dressed alike.

Martin: They might not be able to help themselves.

There's a pause. Martin listens to the music.

Hey, is that . . . Is that Mom? Playing?

Claire: *Listening.* It might be. It's just the radio though.

Martin: You can't tell, just by hearing?

Claire: No. I know the pieces she recorded reasonably well, but my ears aren't educated enough that I can really tell. I have all those private tapes she left, and if I sat down with those I might make some headway. But they're old now and I'm afraid of the wear on them.

Martin: I can have them transferred, you know. I can put them on discs or right onto a computer.

Claire: Well that'd be nice.

Martin: I should probably have them too. I was thinking we should probably play something of hers at the wedding. Then she could be there.

Claire: That'd be lovely. She'd appreciate it.

Martin: She'd have to reconcile herself to the fact that there might be a conga later.

Claire: Really?

Martin: It's a distinct possibility. We're still deciding.

Claire: Can I vote? Because . . . hello . . . conga!

Martin: Claire . . .

Claire: What?

Martin: You're just fantastic.

Claire: I am. Now call your father.

Martin: *Wincing.* Ahhhh, you got me.

She shrugs.

But he might be so uncomfortable . . . at the wedding.

Claire: Squeezing his hands. And that's what your mother would have wanted. *Pause.* I'm joking, of course.

Martin: Yes. I guess you are.

He crosses into a separate light as Claire's light fades.

The idea of my father being uncomfortable at a party really is a bit of a joke. It's because discomfort is the thing he usually brings to the party. It's always been his gift to us.

Walter appears, talking on a cellphone.

Walter: Comp Lit? Is that what you said? That's going to be your major?

Martin: Yes. Comp Lit. Comparative Literature.

Walter: Yes, I know that's what it is. What it means. Okay, I don't exactly know what it is though. I mean . . . what the hell *is* Comparative Literature anyway?

Martin: Well it's . . . the study of literature. Of different languages. Literature that wasn't written in English.

Walter: So you're reading in other languages now? Can you do that?

Leona Brausen as Claire, Andrew MacDonald-Smith as Martin in *Witness to a Conga*

Martin: Not a lot. A little. Well basic French and some German, but no, in Comparative Literature, we mostly read in translations.

Walter: And then what? You read things and then . . . you compare them?

Martin: Well . . . no . . . we analyze . . . I suppose there's some comparison sometimes, but not more than . . . Dad, it's like getting an English degree. You read a lot and you write about what you've read.

Walter: Only it wasn't written in English.

Martin: Exactly.

Walter: Okay, I get that. And your mother's on board with this? Seriously?

Martin: What do you mean, "seriously"? Why wouldn't she be?

Walter: Well statistically, when somebody has a good idea . . .

Martin: I think she's maybe not so much like that . . . now.

Walter: Okay, well I guess I wouldn't really have any way of knowing that. So do you need money? Am I paying for this?

Martin: I don't . . . I don't think so. I think it's all taken care of. It's not like I'm going out of the province or the country or –

Walter: Well, you could. You know, if you wanted to. I would pay for something like that. But you don't ask.

Martin: Well, it's not what I want. I don't want to go . . . somewhere else.

Walter: Yeah, yeah, of course. I was just saying that you could. I could pay for certain things you might want to do. I can't just send money though. That's not how things work.

Martin: Dad, it's fine. I didn't ask for money. I don't need money. I just wanted you know what I'd decided to do. At school.

Walter: Well, good. I hope it all works out and that it stays interesting. You'll probably need to look at something else when you're done that, though, yeah?

Martin: Well, I hadn't quite got –

Walter: I know, I know, you've got to put in your reading time, I get that. But we'll talk again when you're done.

Martin: So . . . in three years . . . we'll talk.

Walter: Okay Martin, you know that's not what I'm saying.

Martin: No, of course I –

Walter: Oh, now, yeah – . . . Looks like my flight's boarding finally.

Martin: Okay, better go.

Walter: Great to catch up, son. Keep me updated on your progress.

Martin: Sure thing. Bye now.

Walter: Bye.

Walter snaps his phone shut and his light goes out.

Martin: You've probably heard about divorced parents who get super competitive about spending money on their children. My parents weren't really like that. I'm not sure if the word exists to describe the condition of "enemies who hate each other too much to even consider fighting." It's like depraved indifference maybe, but there's also something a bit civilized about it.

Pause.

I miss Laura. I'll bet you do too. She's just such a delight. We taught together. That's how we met. Teaching . . . well, not together. Adjacently. Teaching adjacently one evening at a community college.

Martin perches on edge of a table or desk, looking at a paper. Laura approaches.

Laura: Aha, it's just as I thought.

Martin: I beg your pardon?

Laura: You don't have any students. That's why you're able to just sit here and never talk.

Martin: Is that what I do?

Laura: It's what it looks like. I teach across the hall. I look over sometimes and I can just see you through the little window. You're always sitting and looking down or straight ahead, yet while you're doing that I'm always talking. Talking and talking.

Martin: But also looking out the window.

Laura: I may have a problem. So what's your secret?

Martin: This is a writing class. The students are often writing. At the moment they're on a break.

Laura: Oh, okay. That makes sense. You don't make them do assignments at home?

Martin: Sometimes. I like them to discover what they're able to come up with when they don't have time to overthink. I throw something at them and they have at it, then we talk about what they did.

Laura: That's just great. Fun, even. So . . . writing? Creative writing? Is that what this is?

Martin: Actually it's expository writing, which means I get to address grammar and structure. Creativity is encouraged, though.

Laura: And what are people writing about these days?

Martin: Oh . . . the past. A lot of these students are older people who want to write down their great-grand-mother's stories before they forget them.

Laura: That sounds fascinating, maybe.

Martin: Sometimes it is. And sometimes I think "God bless the oral tradition."

Laura: That's certainly more my style.

Martin: Yes now what exactly do *you* talk about, so endlessly across the hall?

Laura: Marketing. I work in advertising and promotions, which means I'm secretly not a teacher. So *Marketing Your Home Business* is what my class is actually called.

Martin: Well that'd explain all the talking. I mean you're not just encouraging people to use their imaginations.

Laura: Well I sort of like to think I am, but yes. There are things like five year plans and targeting specific customers and taking advantage of new media . . . And yet sometimes I just want to say "Marketing your home business? How about selling it? Just sell it and go to work. Look here, folks . . . You don't see *me* doing this and *I'm* an expert."

He laughs.

Well, what a relief to be honest finally. Make no mistake, though, I love this stuff. It's my life's work. My vocation.

Martin: Same here, I guess.

Laura: Reaching into a pocket. Oh hey . . . my card. Handing him a business card. Here ya go.

Martin: Well thanks. Looking at it. Laura.

Laura: Sure thing . . .

Martin: Martin.

Laura: Marty to your friends?

Martin: So far, no.

Laura: Martin, great to have met you, finally. You may not have anything to advertise or promote, in which case you'll need a bit of that creativity to find an alternate reason to make use of the phone number here.

Martin: Okay. I'll give it my best shot.

Laura: See now, that's what I'm really all about.

She exits. He crosses to another light.

Martin: "With womankind, the less we love them,
the easier they become to charm,
the tighter we can stretch above them
enticing nets to do them harm."

That's advice from Pushkin. Good ol' Pushkin. When Pushkin comes to shove . . . I wonder if you can tell who I'm thinking about now.

Music plays quietly as Sheila enters and sits at a desk with papers spread out. Martin turns and looks at her.

"Why did you visit us, but why?
Lost in our backwoods habitation
I'd not have known you, therefore I
would have been spared this laceration."

Time for a pleasant, yet probably ill-advised encounter.

He crosses to Sheila and stands.

Knock knock.

Sheila: Looking up. Martin! What a lovely surprise!

Martin: How are you, Sheila?

Sheila: I'm wonderfully well. I'm grading papers on *Eugene Onegin*.

Martin: Ha! What were the chances? And?

Sheila: Oh Martin, they're terrible. Everybody just wants to tell me the story.

Martin: I guess it's their favourite part.

Sheila: Well then they should be getting it right more often than they do. You'd think when a novel is written in verse that things that happen in it would just stand out a little more. Right? Or is that just . . . me?

Martin: No, I'd say it's me too. But not everyone else.

Sheila: That's discouraging. Actually this one has some promise. Here he actually uses the word "effective."

Martin: Nice. Is he . . . is he like a young me?

Sheila: I'd say a *very* young you. Putting paper aside. I don't want to talk about these things though. Sit down, Martin, and tell me what you've been up to. What brings you by here today?

Martin: Sitting. Well, I actually just came to see you.

Sheila: Oh?

Martin: It's been a while and . . . I have some news.

Sheila: Oh yes? Something career-related? Are you a tenured professor? Have you spit out a book?

Martin: No and no. Sheila, I'm getting married.

Sheila: Even better!

Martin: I thought so.

Sheila: Martin! That's just fantastic. Who is it? Who are you marrying?

Martin: Her name's Laura. You wouldn't have ever met her. But we've been together for . . . oh . . . over a year.

Sheila: That's great. What does she do?

Martin: She's in marketing. Advertising, I mean. Not grocery shopping.

Sheila: Yes, I've learned to make that distinction. And the wedding is to be . . .

Martin: This summer. Mid-July. So . . . we'd like you to come. Do you think that you'd –

Sheila: Oh, of course I'd love to. I'm honoured. Flattered.

Martin: So that's a yes?

Sheila: I . . . only . . . Can you maybe tell me the exact date?

Martin: It's the second Saturday. The 15th, I think. I should just know this as a matter of course, shouldn't I?

Sheila: Well, it's going to be your anniversary for years to come, so sooner is probably better than later. But . . . yes . . . I will have to look up some schedules and things. I know there were some dates in there where I was to be out of town. At a conference . . . unless that was later. Can I get back to you about it?

Martin: Oh, of course. This isn't even the official invitation. You'll be getting something engraved in the mail.

Sheila: Wonderful. And of course if I'm prevented from attending, I just want you to know how much I appreciate being asked.

Martin: Well, you're an important person Sheila. To me.

Sheila: Ohh . . .

Martin: You remember in that first-year class of yours that I took? When you read my paper out as an example of what you were looking for . . .

Sheila: Yes, of course.

Martin: Well if I can just maybe reference Grade Five science for a moment, that was the day my molecules coalesced into solid matter. Up to that point . . .

Sheila: You were gassy?

Martin: I think so. Really annoyingly gassy.

Sheila: Well I was honoured before and now I'm touched. Thank you for telling me that, Martin.

Martin: It's just what's important. I should be on my way now.

Sheila: What, so soon? Indicating papers. I'm not in any hurry to get back to these.

Martin: No. but I do have to go.

Sheila: Right. A man with a fiancée has many obligations.

Martin: Exactly. And I hope you can make the wedding.

Sheila: I'll do my utmost. I'm all curious to meet your Laura. Does she rival Petrarch's, I wonder?

Martin: I choose to think so.

He crosses away from her. She stands and music plays.

Uh-oh.

Sheila: "Love found me all disarmed and found the way was clear to reach my heart down through the eyes which have become the halls and doors of tears."

Martin: Ahhh . . .

He gives a little exasperated shake and Sheila's light and music go out.

Okay, so I've invited the great unattainable love of my life to my wedding. It's the least I can do, right? Since I'm not marrying her. I think it's a given that occasionally in your life you're going to make terrifically bad decisions.

My mom and dad really led by example in that regard. The myriad tests and challenges that make up parenthood didn't faze them at all, for they were able to fail each and every one with breathtaking consistency. I think the pinnacle was the night when I was fourteen years old and they sat me down in the dining room of our magnificent hundred-year-old farm house in upstate New York, and told me it was time for an important talk.

Eleanor and Walter appear seated across from each other at a table. Noble and slightly ominous music plays.

The thing was that the set-up was so great. The three of us at a table . . . That hardly ever happened, and the simple classical formality of it made me think there might be some real stature to the proceedings. Then the talking started.

He sits at the table, between his parents. Music fades.

Eleanor: Martin, I'm glad you have time to speak with us. What we're about to say is very significant.

Martin: Oh? Okay.

Eleanor: And I just want to begin by saying that both your father and I love you very much, and nothing that happens is ever going to change that.

He looks a little puzzled. Walter looks at Eleanor and gestures incredulously and questioningly.

Walter?

Walter: What are you saying that for? That isn't –

Eleanor: I'm saying it because it's true. I want him to know –

Walter: Something like this doesn't need a preamble. The boy probably thinks he did something wrong.

Eleanor: Don't call him the boy, Walter. He's thirteen.

Martin: I'm fourteen.

Eleanor: My point remains.

Walter: Let's pick it up then, shall we? Martin, we love you and you haven't done anything wrong.

Martin: Great.

Eleanor: What we have to tell you is this. Things have been changing between your father and me, and we think it's time we lived apart. So we're separating.

Martin: But . . . what . . .

Eleanor: I know it's probably a shock, but we really have decided to do this and we can't argue about it at this point.

Martin: Oh . . . no . . . I'm not doing that. It's just . . . You've been apart so much already. You're always both traveling on your own all the time and . . .

Eleanor: Yes, and that's not really going to change.

Walter: I don't think he was done, Eleanor.

Eleanor: I'm sorry, Martin. You had something more to say?

Martin: I . . . I don't think I did.

Eleanor: What we're doing is simply admitting that the three of us shouldn't live together as a family and it's in no one's best interest to pretend otherwise. Does that make sense to you?

Martin: Mom, of course it does.

Eleanor: You're not shocked? Upset?

Martin: I . . . um . . .

Walter: Don't prompt him, Eleanor. If he feels something, he can decide what it is and tell you.

Eleanor: Of course. Taking Martin's hand. You don't have to say anything about any of this until you're ready.

Martin: Can I ask some questions?

Eleanor: Of course you can.

Martin: Is this a trial thing? Temporary? Are you going for counseling or anything?

Walter: No, we won't be doing that.

Eleanor: But Martin, if you want to . . . If you need to seek any sort of professional . . . help . . .

Walter gives an exasperated groan and puts one hand on his face.

What? What have I said now?

Walter: Nothing. Never mind.

Eleanor: Walter?

Walter: I don't know what message you're trying to send the – . . . Martin. We love you and it's not your fault but we're divorcing, so you might want to consider getting psychiatric care.

Eleanor: I didn't say –

Martin: Wait, so you're actually divorcing . . . is what you're saying? Not separating. Divorcing.

Walter: Yes. I'm sorry that we weren't clear about that from the outset.

Martin: So we're probably moving. Somebody's moving out, or . . .

Walter: Yes actually. I think we all are.

Eleanor: When things have gone badly in a home, it can be a good time to start over in a new –

Walter: I already have an apartment in the city. I'm going to go and live there because that makes sense to me.

Martin: So I'm staying with Mom?

Eleanor: That's what we're thinking.

Martin: But not here?

Eleanor: No. It's just that I travel so much and yet I play in New York so rarely, and we've only really been here because your father lectures so consistently at –

Martin: So we're going to a different city?

Eleanor: Yes Martin. We'll be moving to Vancouver.

Martin: What? Vancouver??

Martin looks at Walter, who shrugs.

The one in Canada?

Walter: Yes, think of it, son. Socialized medicine and a viable left wing.

Eleanor: Vancouver is really beautiful. I've told you that many times. I always look forward to playing there.

Walter gives a tiny bitter laugh.

It's just a much much healthier place to live.

Walter: Which I'm sure matters to Martin a great deal.

Eleanor: I thought we weren't making assumptions about his feelings.

Walter: Sorry, son.

Martin: Whatever. Pause. Are we done? I have homework.

Eleanor: We can be done for now. I think we've broken the ice and –

Martin: And you're getting a divorce and we're moving to Vancouver. That was today's news.

Eleanor: Are you being glib now, Martin?

Martin: Maybe. I don't know what that means.

Eleanor: If you have any questions about any of this you have to ask them. You have to tell us your thoughts.

Martin: Standing. Okay, I will, but I really –

Walter: Okay look, we're not done. This isn't over. Martin, sit down!

Martin sits.

Eleanor: Walter, I think we *are* done. We don't have to cover absolutely everything tonight and –

Walter: What, you mean we might have to reconvene for more of this hilarity? I don't think so. Martin, your mother has something else to tell you. It has to do with how she selected your new city of residence.

Eleanor: Walter, no. This is for me to talk about in my own time.

Walter: Of course, sorry. That's something I should have known only too well.

Martin: Alright, what . . . now . . . there's something in Vancouver? Mom? Something is . . . some . . . one . . . Is there somebody? Are you . . . You're getting divorced because you're having an affair with somebody . . . in Vancouver?

Walter: Eleanor, look at what your son is having to dredge out of you.

Martin: We're moving to Vancouver because you've met another man?

Eleanor: No!

Martin: Well then . . .

Walter: It's a woman. She's taking you to Vancouver to live with her lesbian lover! That's what all of this is about.

There is a hefty pause.

Martin: Mom?

Eleanor: Martin! Don't you dare look at me that way.

Martin: What?

Eleanor: Oh, I can't take anymore of this.

She gets up and exits. Martin and Walter sit in silence.

Martin: So that's really it? Mom's a lesbian?

Walter: Yup.

Martin: You should probably have let her tell me.

Walter: Yeah, well . . . shoulda woulda coulda . . . Statistically, the odds on her getting around to that point just haven't been too great.

Martin: Do you know when we're moving?

Walter: I have no idea. But I'm gone tomorrow. Getting up. Are you gonna be alright?

Martin: How should I know? I don't know.

Walter: Right. Silly question.

He exits. Martin gets up and crosses to a different light.

Martin: I've never really wanted to live in a jungle. Hunting and gathering for sheer survival seems daunting to me. But there were times in my childhood when I couldn't help thinking, "Mowgli had it pretty good." Raised by wolves. Respectful wolves who'd actively prevent a tiger from eating you. My mom and dad presented their divorce to me in a pretty ridiculous manner. But try as I might, I can't see that there was a downside to that event. I mean . . . I got a parent out of it, finally.

He crosses and sits with Eleanor. Claire enters with glasses of iced tea on a tray.

Claire: Here we are. Iced tea. I make my own, so it might be less sweet than you're used to, so there's the sugar.

Eleanor: Taking a glass. Thanks, Claire.

Martin: Taking a glass. Thank you.

He starts to put a heaping spoonful of sugar in his glass.

Eleanor: Martin, taste it first. You don't need all that –

Martin: Mom, she said –

Eleanor: It's just a lot of sugar.

Claire: And he's a teenager, Eleanor. It's what they like.

Eleanor: That doesn't mean it's good for them.

Claire: I think they do actually need it, in some cases.

Martin: There we go.

He puts the sugar in and stirs.

Claire: And I have some cookies. I'll be right back.

She exits.

Eleanor: Martin, I'm just going to say this quickly. Please don't overdo it with the cookies.

Martin: What do you mean?

Eleanor: Don't eat all of them. Even if Claire and I don't take them, they're not all for you.

Martin: What the . . . What's wrong with you? You're acting like . . .

Eleanor: Like a mother?

Martin: Yeah, you don't need to do that.

Eleanor: I beg your pardon?

Martin: You don't have to put a show on for your girlfriend.

Eleanor: What? When did you start talking to me this way?

Martin: Sorry. It's all the sugar.

Claire enters with cookies.

Claire: Here we are. Oatmeal chocolate chip.

Eleanor: Taking one. Claire, did you bake these?

Claire: I did. Offering Martin a cookie. Martin?

Martin: I'd better not.

Eleanor: Martin, take a cookie.

Martin: No thanks. Not just now.

Claire: Putting down the plate. Well I'll leave them right here.

She sits.

So you're settling in at your school, Martin?

Martin: I guess so. It's big.

Claire: It's an adjustment, I guess. To be in a public school after being in a private –

Martin: It's school. It's the same.

Eleanor has taken a sip of her tea. She winces and adds more sugar.

Claire: Do you have a favourite subject?

Martin shrugs.

Eleanor: He loves English. He likes to read.

Claire: Yes, I guess I actually knew that. Your mother really has told me a lot about you, Martin.

Martin: Really? Then you must have asked a lot of questions.

Eleanor sighs a little and rolls her eyes.

Claire: Well . . . yes . . . I suppose I . . . I just do that.

Eleanor: Looking at her watch. Oh look, three o'clock. I have to practice for fifteen minutes.

Claire: What? Right now?

Martin: Oh yeah.

Eleanor: Your piano is . . .

Claire: In the other room. Like always.

Eleanor: Right. Well . . . carry on. Enjoy your tea.

She exits.

Claire: Did I say something?

Martin: I don't know.

Claire: Hm.

She eats her cookie, a little absently. The piano is heard in the other room.

Oh . . . it never sounded like that when I played it. I had lessons about thirty years ago, but they didn't take. It was my grandmother's piano though, so I could never really bear to part with it. I thought it was a good place for knick-knacks, but I've recently been enlightened in that regard.

Martin: I'll bet you have.

Claire: After a pause. Martin, is there anything you want to know about me?

Martin: I don't think so . . . really.

Claire: Well, if there ever is . . . don't hesitate to ask. Me, I mean. Not your mom.

Martin: Sure.

There's a pause.

Okay, here's something. A little question.

Claire: Go ahead.

Martin: What . . . exactly . . . is it you like so much about my mother? You're in love with her, right? So tell me why.

Claire: Wow. That's quite a request.

Martin: Shouldn't it be easy to answer?

Claire: You'd think. But I'm certainly not going to.

Martin: But you said –

Claire: I know what you're doing, Martin. You want me to sputter out a few sincere things, and then you'll use your lifetime of experience to refute them. You might do it bluntly, or you might just roll your eyes behind my back, but the intention is the same. You want, in some tiny way, to hurt me, and I don't think it's because you even dislike me. So how much sense does *that* make? I'll tell ya. None. I would never want to hurt you, intentionally or otherwise. I've made you tea and cookies. I want things to be pleasant . . . all the time . . . so that we can converse freely about interesting things that we know and that we experience. So that means no hurting. No you hurting me, no me hurting you. Is that clear?

He nods a little, then bursts into tears.

Oh-oh. Oh no . . . Now I seem to have –

Martin: No, it's fine. Thank you Claire.

She gestures questioningly and he nods, so she slides over and embraces him. They sit for a moment.

Claire: You do want a cookie, don't you?

Martin: Claire, I want all of them.

The light fades on them and Martin gets up and crosses to another area.

If I *had* actually bothered to ask anything about Claire, I might have known that she was a junior high school teacher. She taught Grade Eight, so I'd never really had a chance. Wiping his eyes a little. That was emotional. Thank God my mother was playing Mozart throughout, or things might have gone completely off the rails. Well judged, Mom, well judged indeed.

Eleanor: Appearing in a separate light. Thank you Martin. It's a treat to hear you say something like that.

Martin: Well, credit where it's due . . .

Eleanor: You're just usually going on about my *poor* judgment, till I almost start to believe myself that I –

Martin: Mom, there's a really good reason for that. Why, not two years ago –

Eleanor: Oh, rub it in.

Walter appears with a phone.

Walter: Hello, Walter here.

Martin: Dad, hi. It's Martin.

Walter: Martin . . . This is unexpected. How are things? How are you doing?

Martin: Uh . . . not great, Dad. I have to tell you something.

Walter: Oh?

Martin: Are you . . . somewhere quiet? Are you alone right now?

Walter: I'm just in my office. What –

Martin: Dad, it's about Mom. She was in an accident. This morning.

Walter: An accident? What kind of –

Martin: A car accident. A collision. She was driving and she shouldn't have –

Walter: She was driving? Your mother was driving? I didn't think she could anymore.

Martin: Well, she didn't usually. She wasn't supposed to, and she knew that.

Walter: She shouldn't have been driving! Why would she –

Martin: Well, she had some good days when her hands just seemed normal, and so she probably –

Walter groans in exasperation.

But she obviously lost control because she apparently drove right into oncoming traffic and then –

Walter: What kind of vehicle was she in?

Martin: What? What does that matter?

Walter: I don't know. I'm just trying to picture what –

Martin: It was an SUV. It was Claire's SUV.

Walter: So that might have helped things at least?

Martin: Yeah, but no. No.

Walter: Alright, so . . . what? Tell me what happened? How is she?

Martin: Dad . . . she . . . died. Mom died. Almost right away.

Walter: She's . . . dead? She's . . . Why didn't you say that first?

Martin: I don't know. I just wanted to explain –

Walter: Yeah, no, I'm sorry. Look . . . Martin . . . What can I do? What do you want me to do?

Martin: I don't . . . Nothing . . . I just wanted you to know. I wanted to tell you.

Walter: Do you want me to come out there?

Martin: No, you don't have to do that. There's no reason . . . there's nothing . . . nothing . . .

Walter: Pause. Hello? Martin? Are you still there?

Martin: Yeah, yeah . . . sorry. I think I need to go. I gotta sit down and –

Walter: Of course, yes. Do what you need to. But call me if you need to tell me anything else. About anything else. I suppose . . . there'll be a funeral?

Martin: Yeah, I don't know anything about that yet. Probably next week sometime.

Walter: Right.

Martin: But don't think you have to come for it. No one would expect that. She wouldn't.

Walter: Well okay, but if you want me to . . . I could . . .

Martin: Dad, we'll just talk about another time, okay? I'll call you soon.

Walter: Alright, good. You should do that.

Martin: Bye-bye.

Walter: Bye.

Walter's light goes out. Martin turns to Eleanor.

Martin: You shouldn't have been driving, Mom.

Eleanor: It was only five blocks. Five blocks there and five blocks back. My hands were fine. It was Claire's birthday and I was just picking up her cake. I didn't want her to have to pick up her own cake.

Martin: You could have asked someone else. Anyone who knows Claire would have done that for you.

Eleanor: I don't like calling in favours. It's time-consuming.

Martin: Right. And now you've got all the time in the world.

Eleanor: I wanted to do it myself. My hands were fine. I thought I could do it. For Claire.

Martin: You don't think she'd maybe have been a little ticked off?

Eleanor: You don't need to make things any more unpleasant than they were. I'll tell you this though . . . When I was dangling there . . . strapped into a Jimmy and covered in cake, with the life force seeping out of me . . . all I could think was . . . at least I died in an act of love.

Martin: Mm-hm. Mixed with some impatience.

Eleanor: Now why would you say a thing like that to your poor dead mother?

Martin: Because I know she'll never ever hear it.

Eleanor's light goes out.

Do you know who's got consistently good judgment? Laura. My fiancée. You never find yourself looking at *her* and saying "You did *what?*"

Laura enters with a shoulder bag or large purse. As she approaches Martin, his light expands.

Here she is right now, and see how everything's just immediately brightening up?

Laura: Darling!

Martin: Laura! My Laura!

They kiss.

I've missed you.

Laura: Wonderful. And look what I have.

She takes a box of engraved envelopes out of her bag.

Invitations!

Martin: Are those ours?

Laura: Indeed, and they're all addressed and sealed and ready to go.

Martin: So this really is it? Last chance to bail?

Laura: Mm, no, given what these cost.

Martin: Alright, good. I'm always happy when a decision has been made *for* me.

Laura: All that remains is for them to be stamped and mailed. I'll let you do that, and then it'll be like you helped.

Martin: Perfect. Taking the invitations and stamps. This is all of them?

Laura: Yes. Well, actually, all but one.

Martin: Oh?

Laura: I . . . hand-delivered it.

Martin: Is that allowed? I guess it was to someone you see all the time.

Laura: Yeah, not exactly. Pause. It was your friend Sheila's invitation. I stopped by her office.

Martin: You did *what?*

Sheila appears, seated at her desk, perusing an essay. Laura approaches her.

Laura: Excuse me, Ms Waverly?

Sheila: Looking up. Hello? Yes?

Laura: Hi. We haven't met, but I'm . . . well, I'm just here to invite you to my wedding.

Sheila: Well, how delightful and unexpected.

Laura: I know! Actually, I'm Martin Lowell's fiancée. I'm –

Sheila: Laura!

Laura: Yes! You've heard of me. That's . . . good . . .

Sheila: I've remembered your name, thanks to a literary reference.

Laura: Oh, handy. Was it by chance . . . *Little House on the Prairie?*

Sheila: No, it was something else. But yes, Martin was actually here last week and told me of your engagement, and that the wedding was imminent. You must be very excited.

Laura: I am. *Handing over an envelope.* So here's your invitation.

Sheila: Well, thank you so much. Are you . . . delivering them all by hand?

Laura: Sheila, I'm not.

Sheila: No? Then I guess I'm especially honoured.

She smiles a little questioningly at Laura.

Laura: Alright, I'll be honest with you. We're not having a very big wedding, and other than relatives and mutual friends of Martin's and mine . . . Well, you're basically the only person invited who I've never met. I didn't want to get all preoccupied with that, so I thought I'd put a face to the name and –

Sheila: Of course, of course. That makes good sense. It's your wedding and you should know who's going to be there.

Laura: Exactly. So . . . you were a . . . teacher of Martin's?

Sheila: Yes. I taught him in one of his first-year undergraduate classes, and then I was his advisor when he did his honours degree. I didn't really realize that I'd been particularly influential in his academic career, but I guess . . . *Pause.* We never dated. We were never involved at that level of –

Laura: Oh no, I certainly didn't mean to imply . . . or ask . . .

Sheila: Well no, but aren't you glad you don't have to?

Laura: *Laughing.* Yes. Thank you.

Sheila: *Laughing also.* You're welcome.

Laura: Well alright then. I hope I'll see you at the big event.

Sheila: *Hesitantly.* Yes . . . ahhh . . .

Laura: You don't want to come? You have something else to do? *Pause.* It's really none of my business.

Sheila: Well no, it's important. You're planning a major catered event and you've been good enough to invite me and . . . *Looking at the invitation.* I know I'm not doing anything in particular at that time . . .

Laura: But . . .

Sheila: I really cannot attend. I shouldn't.

Laura gestures questioningly.

I think that if I told you my reasons, you would concur. I would just feel very awkward about sharing this information with Martin.

They look at each other intently for a moment. The light fades and Laura crosses back to Martin.

Martin: So did she tell you?

Laura: She did.

Martin: And it's an acceptable excuse?

Laura: I'd say so.

Martin: And you promised never to tell me?

Laura: She didn't make me do that. It's at my discretion, since presumably I know you better than she does.

Martin: Right, and now you know *her* better than I do too, so . . .

Laura: I can tell you, Martin. If it's really important to you to know why she won't be there . . .

Martin: I'm feeling that it is.

Laura: After a pause. Alright . . . Well . . . the winter before last . . . January, I guess . . . Your father was in town. And you were showing him around some of the university buildings.

Martin: Oh . . . Yes . . .

He crosses and joins Walter in another area.

Walter: Looking up. Well . . . it's impressive . . . architecturally. But I don't know how anybody learns anything with all this space and light bearing down on them.

Martin: Well it *is* an uncharacteristically sunny day for this time of year. When things are properly overcast, the windows really don't hesitate to share that with us.

Walter: Then I suppose it's alright.

Martin: Said with profound conviction.

Walter: Oh, I'm not disparaging your education. I'm sure you learned a lot here. And it's not like we're outdoors. Completely. Distastefully. You know, in Arizona, for example –

Martin: Oh.

Walter: What? Stop? Stop talking?

Martin: No, sorry Dad, I just saw someone I know.

He waves off.

Walter: Oh. *Turning.* Ohhh . . .

Sheila enters.

Martin: Sheila, hi.

Sheila: Hello there, Martin. It's nice to see you back in these parts.

Martin: Thanks. I'm just here giving my father a bit of a tour.

Sheila: Oh, nice.

Martin: Dad, Sheila here was one of my teachers and colleagues when I was doing my Comp Lit degree. Sheila Waverly, Walter Lowell.

Walter: *Shaking her hand.* Professor Waverly, it's nice to meet you.

Sheila: Mr. Lowell.

Martin: *Out of one side of his mouth.* Doctor.

Sheila: Oh, I'm sorry, Doctor –

Walter: Walter is just fine.

Sheila: Wait . . . Walter Lowell . . . I saw that on a . . . handbill, or something . . .

Martin: Dad was just in town to give a lecture. For the Political Science Department.

Sheila: Right, but . . . that was a major event, wasn't it? With snacks afterward?

Walter: I wouldn't have it otherwise.

Sheila: Well, I'm sorry I missed it. I just never thought to connect the two of you on account of the name.

Walter: It's not so uncommon, I suppose.

Sheila: And are you liking our campus?

Walter: Yes. It's so bright. Spacious. Not like the dank fox-holes of learning back east.

Sheila: Oh, don't I know from dank.

Walter: Yes, so you're obviously from –

Martin: Looking at his watch. Oh, Dad, sorry to interrupt, but I think we'd better go. I didn't realize how late it had gotten and I have to catch a bus.

Walter: Alright, well it'd be a shame to not do *that*. But . . . you can just go. I can make my way back to the hotel. And I wouldn't mind having a look at the library while I'm here.

Martin: Well, if you think . . . I mean . . . okay. Can you find your way to the elevators? And out?

Sheila: I can show him. It's no trouble.

Walter: Why, thank you.

Martin: Okay, well, great. Thanks, Sheila. See ya, Dad, I guess.

Walter: Good-bye, Martin.

Martin turns and exits.

Sheila: So . . . you wanted to go the library . . . or down to the –

Walter: Oh, neither.

She looks at him quizzically.

Sheila, I'd like to buy you dinner. May I do that?

Sheila: Oh heavens . . . why?

Walter: You don't think you're deserving?

She laughs.

I was disappointed in the Political Science Department. Those people weren't quite . . . on. I'd really like a more pleasant conclusion to my visit here, and I don't have anyone else to –

Sheila: You aren't seeing Martin again? Later.

Walter: No. That was it.

Sheila: Not a terribly emotional farewell you had. Though it isn't my place to –

Walter: No, I admire your candor. Martin's not terribly comfortable with that sort of thing.

Sheila: You know . . . I'm not either.

Walter: Well, that makes three of us. So with one gone, things just have to be a little more relaxed.

Sheila: I . . .

Walter: So what do you say? Are we on?

Sheila: Probably . . . I just need to know . . . Do you have strong opinions about literature?

Walter: I'm not sure that I –

Sheila: Do you read fiction? At all?

Walter: Never.

Sheila: I'll get my coat.

Their light fades. Light comes up on Martin and Laura.

Martin: So he took her to dinner? And because of that –

Laura: No. There's more.

Martin: Turning away. Oh . . . no . . . really?

Laura: Maybe I've said enough.

Martin: No, I think I need to hear it all. I'll make it out worse in my head if you don't finish.

Laura: Yeeeah . . . I don't know about that.

Martin: Just tell me. Just say it.

Laura: Well . . . they started an affair. That night . . . and in the following weeks.

Martin: Here?

Laura: No, I think mostly in New York. She'd go there on weekends. They may have gone other places too. In the middle, between here and there.

Martin: And they deliberately kept it a secret from me?

Laura: From everyone, I think, from the sound of it. And it was over before long, anyway. It all fell apart. In Venice.

Martin: What?

Laura: In Venice . . . they broke up.

Martin: Venice? In Italy?

Laura: Yes. He took her there . . . for the Carnival.

Martin: What?

Laura: They went to a bunch of . . . balls. Masquerades. Carnival things.

He turns and stares at her incredulously.

People do that . . . apparently.

Martin: I just . . . Balls? I didn't . . . know he knew any . . . Venetian nobility . . . or . . . So what happened?

Laura: All I know is that in the middle of it all they had some sort of big fight and it was just over.

Martin: A fight?

Laura: Yeah . . . knock-down drag-out is how she put it and I don't know if that was literal or –

Martin: Okay, that's good, that's good, that's enough.

Laura: It's also all I got. But you can maybe see why she'd be reluctant to come to the wedding if he was going to –

Martin: Yes. Yes. Yes.

The light around Martin fades abruptly, isolating him. Music begins to build behind him and he runs his fingers through his hair rather feverishly.

My unattainable love and my unavailable father have had an affair. How's that for a kick in the head? And the worst of it might well be that they did it with no malice toward me whatsoever, which just makes it a senseless horrible random thing, and you can say that at least they got some sort of spectacular comeuppance for it, except it's going to be in my head forever now, the two of them trying to kill each other at some ball in Venice, and as vile a thing as that is to suddenly have to live with, I can't help noting that somebody finally stepped up to the music.

The music gets much louder. Walter and Sheila appear, elegantly dressed and masked, she in a full-skirted ballgown. As the music thunders away, they have an almost balletic confrontation, with fevered embracing, shoving, clutching, and chasing, ending in his dragging her across the floor and out of sight. Martin stands wide-eyed and horrified, till music goes out abruptly and a light change puts him back with Laura.

Laura: Martin . . . Martin! I'm still here.

Martin: Sorry . . . what . . .

Laura: Nothing, just . . . I'm here. But I think I'm going to go. You may want to be alone with all this new information.

Martin: Yeah, Laura, I'm sorry, I don't know, I . . .

Laura: Maybe I shouldn't have gone to see her. But I did. And I think we're probably better off knowing what we do.

Martin: Yes. Somebody's been spared something. Definitely.

Laura: Sorry to have to ask, but . . . have you even talked to your dad? About the wedding?

Martin: I haven't.

Laura: Looking through invitations. Here's his invitation. I don't want to just mail it if you haven't –

Martin: Taking it. Yeah, I'll take it.

Laura: What are you going to do with –

Martin: I'm going to go see him. In New York.

Laura: You're going to deliver it?

Martin: That may be what happens.

Their light fades and he crosses to a tightly lit area. An ominous trumpet call sounds as he stands and stares straight ahead. Light comes up on Walter, sitting at a table with a cup of coffee. Martin's light fades and he crosses to Walter.

Martin: Dad, hi. Sorry if I made you wait. I missed the –

Walter: It's alright. I have nowhere to be.

Martin: Sitting. Okay, great.

Walter: It's good to see you, son. A surprise, certainly.

Martin: Yeah. I'll bet it is.

They shake hands, just a little awkwardly.

Walter: Where are you staying?

Martin: At a hotel. Near Grand Central. I'm just here for a day, really.

Walter: Oh yeah? For a job interview?

Martin: Uh . . . no. Dad, I just needed to talk to *you*.

Walter: Oh?

Martin: Yes . . . about a couple of things.

Walter: And you didn't want to just phone?

Martin: No. No, Dad, I didn't. I don't . . . I don't like talking on the phone with you.

Walter raises an eyebrow.

It's because there are silences sometimes and I don't know what they mean. I can't have that with what I need to talk to you about today.

Walter: Alright. I suppose I understand that. But . . . did you want to order anything? Before we –

Martin: No. Maybe later. Maybe not . . .

There's a pause. Walter calmly indicates that he's not about to speak.

Dad, I'm getting married.

Walter: What? That's great! That's what you have to tell me? That's great! Isn't it? If it's what you want . . .

Martin: Yes, of course it is, absolutely.

Walter: But . . . who to? Is it someone I'd . . . No, I'm sure I have no idea.

Martin: You haven't met. Her name's Laura. We've been together for just over a year. She's fantastic.

Walter: As she should be. So . . . when –

Martin: In July. The middle of July.

Walter: Well, that's good. That's soon but not too soon. I know I won't be doing much of any – . . . Or . . . maybe I'm presuming.

Martin: *After a little pause.* Yeah . . . we need to table that topic for a moment.

Walter: Alright. *Pause.* The floor is still yours.

Martin: Dad . . . I learned something recently. Something pretty upsetting. About you and Sheila Waverly.

Walter: *After a little pause.* Ah. She told you.

Martin: No, but I found out just the same. And I know that what happened was unpleasant enough that she won't come to the wedding if you're there.

Walter: So you're telling me that I won't be –

Martin: No! That's not it at all! I want to know why, Dad. I want to know why you did that?

Walter: "That"? What? Why did I have an affair with that gorgeous and sophisticated woman? Because I could. Because I can. Because I wanted to. And she wanted to. *Pause.* You think it had something to do with you?

Martin: How could it not?

Walter: She told me you weren't that close. That she rarely saw you since you graduated.

Martin turns away, wincing.

What is she to you? What is your personal stake here, Martin? If you're marrying this Laura, why are you –

Martin: Turning back. No! You're not asking questions! I'm doing that.

Walter: Fine. That's fine.

He sits back, and takes a sip of his coffee.

Martin: It ended badly. Your affair ended badly . . . in Venice. I want to know about that.

Walter: Alright. Are there specific details you –

Martin: Did you hurt her?

Walter: I think we hurt each other pretty well. Or . . . do you mean physically?

Martin: Yes. That's what I mean.

Walter: I don't think so, I know we hurt our hotel room somewhat. And there was shouting. Slamming. I won't say violence wasn't in the air. But the details . . . everything that was said . . . I actually don't remember a word of it.

Martin: What?

Walter: I had had so much to drink that I really can't recall anything specific that was said. That's how it was the next morning, and that's how it remains. I know it all began down in the ballroom when I saw her talking for extended periods with other men. That much

I can certainly remember, and also going back to our room by myself and ordering a bottle of vodka and then . . .

He shrugs.

Martin: She left that night?

Walter: She did. I woke up and found a note. "You're a drunk," is what it said. "Get help." That was all.

Martin: So . . .

Walter: Is she right? Do I have a drinking problem?

Martin nods.

Martin, I don't. I drink very rarely. But I can understand why she'd have thought that. The whole time I was with her, we both . . . Well, it's a means to an end, isn't it. Once you've realized you don't have a whole lot of common ground . . .

There's a pause.

No more questions? Maybe I'll just keep going. I did, in fact, end up doing what she recommended. You wake up alone on the floor of a hotel room that's costing you a thousand euro a night, surrounded by broken lamps and carnival masks . . . and you realize that that's just so remarkable that you'd at least like to tell someone about it. But there isn't anybody. You can't think of anybody in your life that you tell that sort of thing to. And that means maybe . . . it's time you went to see a mental health professional.

Martin: So you've done that?

Walter: Yes.

Martin: And?

Walter: Oh, all cured. All better. Pause. Our work is ongoing. But I'm enjoying it.

Martin: Well, I suppose I wish I'd known –

Walter: Well, yes, telling you about it has been on my "to do" list, which is an official thing that we review and –

Martin: And now it doesn't have to be anymore.

Walter: Hooray. And here's a fun thing: I think I don't hate your mother anymore.

Martin: Well that's good. Timely.

Walter: I know, I know, but we take progress where it comes.

Martin: Can I ask how you managed to –

Walter: To overcome? I did a certain amount of remembering. Out loud. What I came to recall is that when I first met Eleanor, I thought she was basically . . . unattainable perfection. And the unattainable aspect was what really enchanted me most, and made me want to fight to have her. And she let me get closer and closer till finally I seemed to have actually won her . . . but there was always this distance, a look in her eyes or . . . the absence of one actually . . . that said I still hadn't completely got to her. I thought it might just take years of perseverance, but as time went on, that little distance between us just grew and grew, till of course finally the thing I learned was that I never really could have had her at all.

Martin: So you were resentful?

Walter: Yes. Understandably so, I'd hope. But in choosing to be preoccupied with the unattainable aspect of her, I never quite got free of the notion of her being perfect, and that made me want to wound her. Pause. This is probably not making much sense really, but –

Martin: No, I actually do get it. But Mom *wasn't* perfect. She was a pretty big bowl o' nuts a lot of the time. If I'd known you just needed some reassurance about that –

Walter: Martin, being nuts doesn't preclude perfection.

Martin: No, I guess there are other forces that take care of that for us.

Light fades on them and comes up on Eleanor, seated on the floor holding her arms out in front of her, her palms turned upward. She's trembling a little and wincing. Martin approaches behind her.

Martin: Mom . . . People are waiting. They want to see you.

Eleanor: I can't go out there. I won't.

Martin: But they've been so patient and –

Eleanor: No, I just can't . . .

Martin: Mom, why are you on the floor?

Eleanor: Where's Claire? I need to see Claire.

Martin: She's just outside. She's –

Eleanor: Get Claire! Get her . . .

Claire: Entering. Lennie, what's going on? Why haven't you . . . What are you doing on the floor?

Martin: She's just sitting here. She says won't see anyone.

Claire: Alright, I've got it. Martin, thank you. I'll –

Martin: Yeah, I'll just let you . . .

Leona Brausen as Claire, Sheri Somerville as Eleanor in *Witness to a Conga* (photo by Andrew MacDonald-Smith)

He backs away without exiting. Claire kneels beside Eleanor.

Claire: Lennie, what is it? I know you need your alone time after you play, but . . . You shouldn't be on the floor. Let me help you up here . . .

She reaches for her arms. Eleanor winces and pulls away.

Eleanor: No, don't touch my arms . . . don't touch my hands . . . They hurt so much.

Claire: Oh . . . Eleanor . . .

There's a long pause. Eleanor looks at Claire, then lowers her head.

It's worse, isn't it . . . Things haven't gotten better.

Eleanor shakes her head.

They never did, probably, right? Not after any of those treatments.

Eleanor shakes her head.

And you just . . . soldiered on?

Eleanor: I have to stop. Claire, I have to stop.

Claire: Of course you do. You can cancel engagements for as long as you need to.

Eleanor: No. I just have to be done. I'm never going to get better.

Claire: Well, if you don't play, then maybe there's a chance that you'll recover certain –

Eleanor: No. I meant I'm never going to get better at playing. It's the only thing I could ever count on . . . but now that's not going to be possible . . . so I want to stop. I don't want to hurt like this ever again, but more than that . . . I don't want to start going backward.

The pain will *always* subside, but going backward is something you just can't –

Claire: Overlapping. Then you'll stop. You're stopping. You've stopped. Pause. Lennie, it's over.

Eleanor: Oh . . . thank you Claire . . .

Claire embraces her gingerly around the shoulders.

Claire: But just . . . Rock bottom doesn't have to look as bad as it feels, so please . . . let's just get you into a chair.

With a little awkward effort, she helps Eleanor to a chair, and kneels beside her.

And I don't like you saying that there was only one thing you could count on.

Eleanor: Oh, you know I didn't mean –

Claire: No, of course you didn't.

Eleanor: You're going to be seeing a lot more of me. Around the house.

Claire: You won't hear me objecting to that.

Eleanor: I won't be the same. I know I won't. I'll be a different person. I can't even say what I'll be like and –

Claire: It's fine. I like to meet new people. And . . . the outer wrapping won't look any less tasty . . .

Claire gives Eleanor a little kiss.

Eleanor: Please . . . my son's just outside.

Martin: Actually, Mom, I'm right here.

Eleanor: Oh . . . no . . .

Martin: Mom, I'm proud of you. This must be so hard.

Eleanor: Thank you, Martin. I'm glad I won't have to tell you now. I'm terrible at that sort of thing. Pause. I wish we could go.

Martin: I can tell these people you can't see them. I'll send them away.

Eleanor: No, they've waited. They deserve something. Tell them if they send their programs in I'll sign them.

Martin: But Mom, how could you, with your –

Eleanor: Oh, Claire will do it. She never minds.

Claire: It's true.

Eleanor: Now go on. Make sure you get a pen.

Martin exits and the light fades on Eleanor and Claire, smiling at one another. Light comes up on Martin and Walter as before.

Walter: And she never played again after that?

Martin: Not a note. Well maybe a little in someone's lesson, but not in public and never at home.

Walter: I didn't know she taught.

Martin: Yeah, she did, and you know . . . this is interesting: At her funeral . . . a lot of Mom's piano students came. She'd only taught for about four years, and it wasn't something she spoke of particularly, except to imply that there was usually something she'd rather be doing instead. But there were a still a good number of these students there and they mostly sat together . . . and they all cried *so hard*. People were crying generally all over, but this one little section of pews was just really gasping and choking and sobbing, to the point where both

Claire and I almost started to laugh. Though we didn't, in mother's memory. But afterward, all of those students came up to us and said . . . that Mom was the kindest, funniest, most patient and encouraging person that they had ever met.

They look at each other.

Walter: See? Perfect to the end.

Martin: The best teacher they ever had.

He looks away for a moment then turns back to Walter.

Dad, I don't know you very well . . . but I'm quite certain that I want you to have this.

He hands Walter the wedding invitation.

Walter: It's . . . Looks at it, then at Martin. You're sure?

Martin: Yes, I am. I want you to come. Sheila won't be attending.

Walter: You shouldn't un-invite her on my account.

Martin: No, it's fine. I don't want her there.

Walter: Alright. Looking at the invitation. July 15th. I'm looking forward to it.

Martin: Good.

Walter: It's our best shot, isn't it?

Martin: Better not look at it that way. Pause. You know, Dad . . . I do have one more question . . . about Venice.

Walter: Uh-oh.

Martin: Who do you *know* there? How did you get invited to all those balls?

Walter: Invited? You don't get invited. You buy tickets.

Martin: Seriously? Where?

Walter: From a travel agent. Or online. I went to the American Express office.

Martin: Oh . . . Puzzled and incredulous. That's just so . . .

The light starts to fade on them. Martin gets up and walks forward into his own spotlight.

Well, I guess there's always going to be something new to be disappointed about. Actually, that was pretty satisfying. My dad is coming to the wedding and Sheila's not and that's how it ought to be. Sheila . . . I wonder what she'll do instead. On July 15th. I guess I'm still thinking about her.

Sheila appears in a separate light, holding a book, slowly flipping through pages.

But maybe there's a difference.

He turns and looks at her.

Yes. There is. Do you hear that? Pause. Nothing. Nothing except . . .

Sheila's light fades and she walks away slowly. Martin listens till her receding footsteps are no longer heard. He pauses another moment before speaking.

The orchestra may be gone. I wonder if I'll miss it.

Soft music is heard. It's Latin in character, and a bit sultry.

Oh . . . wait now . . . what's that? That's something I haven't heard before. It's definitely an orchestra, but . . . I wonder what . . . Turning. Ohh . . .

Laura enters. She has a large flower in her hair and sways gently to the rhythm of the music.

A new development.

Laura: I'm spending a little time with your musician friends, Martin. I think you may have underestimated the breadth of their repertoire.

Martin: Are they playing a . . .

Laura: Funny thing. It seems we never really had a choice. It was out of our hands.

Claire enters, swaying in a similar manner.

Claire: There's always been a conga, Martin. There's always going to be one, and who's in it may never be entirely up to you.

Laura: But it's yours, Martin It's your conga and that means you don't ever get to sit it out.

Walter, Eleanor, and Sheila also appear, swaying on the periphery.

Martin: Stop watching and get into line? Is that what you're saying?

Claire: Better even. The thing about this conga is that *you* get to lead it.

Martin: Ahh . . .

Music abruptly slams into high gear, simultaneously swelling and speeding up.

CONGAAAA!!!

Martin steps into action, crossing the stage and interacting first with Laura, then with all the others in turn. Everyone is swept up in the pounding rhythms and they move together tantalizingly, then apart. Martin does a few more steps with Laura, then the others fall into line, each decisively putting hands on the hips of the person in front of them. Martin takes his place at the front of the line.

Blackout.

PLAYOGRAPHY

All These Heels 1982
(co-written with Phil Zyp)
The Unremembered Budapest 1984
Dinah's Wine Bar 1984
(composer Gary Lloyd)
Chicks Akimbo 1985
Women in Bed 1985
My Miami Melody 1985
(composers Gary Lloyd and R.J. Smart)
The Vile Governess & Other Psychodramas 1986
What Gives? 1986
(composers Gary Lloyd and R.J. Smart)
Cocktails at Pam's 1986
Neck-Breaking Car-Hop 1987
Swiss Pajamas 1988
Hopscotch Holiday 1988
(composers Gary Lloyd and R.J. Smart)
Damp Fury 1988
Teens in Togas 1989
(composer Gary Lloyd)
When Girls Collide 1989
All Ears 1989
Planet of the Lost Swing Babes 1990
(composer Gary Lloyd)
The Glittering Heart 1990
The Swift Hotel 1990
The Hothouse Prince 1991

The Jazz Mother 1991
A Night With Barbara 1991
The Spanish Abbess of Pilsen 1992
Two Tall, Too Thin 1992
The Argentine Picnic & Other Lemoine Vignettes 1992
Shockers Delight! 1993
The Book of Tobit 1993
The Delightful Garden of Saint Piquillo 1994
The Visitation of the Paragon 1994
Connie in Egypt 1994
The Noon Witch 1995
The River Princess and the Frozen Town 1995
Evelyn Strange 1995
Fall Down, Go Boom: A Skater's Tragedy 1996
Fatty Goes to College 1996
The Velvet Shock 1996
The Lake of the Heart 1997
Fatty's Big Show 1997
Ludicrous Pie 1997
Pith! 1997
Whiplash Weekend! 1997
The Subject of My Affections 1998
The Rules of Irene 1998
Tales of the Electress 1998
(co-written with Trevor Anderson)
Fever-Land 1999
Fatty Goes Wild 1999
Skirts on Fire 2000
Orlando Unhinged 2001
On the Banks of the Nut 2001
Eros and the Itchy Ant 2002
(musical sequence composed by Ryan Sigurdson)
The Exquisite Hour 2002
Vidalia 2002

Caribbean Muskrat 2003
(co-written with Josh Dean)
The Margin of the Sky 2003
The Salon of the Talking Turk 2005
A Momentary Lapse 2005
(co-written with Jocelyn Ahlf)
A Grand Time in the Rapids 2005
At the Zenith of the Empire 2005
Hey, Countess! 2006
East of My Usual Brain 2007
Revenge of the South Sea Bubble 2008
A Rocky Night for His Nibs 2008
Happy Toes 2008
The Addlepated Nixie 2009
Mother of the Year 2009
The Oculist's Holiday 2009
The Seersucker Toady 2010
The Ambassador's Wives 2010
Witness to a Conga 2010
The Scent of Compulsion 2011
Mrs. Lindeman Proposes… 2011
The Hoof and Mouth Advantage 2011
(co-written with Jocelyn Ahlf)

Photo by Andrew MacDonald-Smith. Photographed at Somerville Wine Room, Edmonton.

Stewart Lemoine has been writing and directing for Teatro La Quindicina in Edmonton, Alberta since 1982 and is the author of over sixty plays, including *Cocktails at Pam's, Evelyn Strange, Neck-Breaking Car-Hop, Shockers Delight!, The Margin of the Sky, Pith!, At the Zenith of the Empire, The Ambassador's Wives, Mother of the Year,* and *The Vile Governess and Other Psychodramas.* He's long been a mainstay of the Edmonton Fringe Theatre Festival, and has premiered twenty works there since the event's inception. Since 1994, he and Teatro have been resident at Edmonton's Varscona Theatre, and their productions have also been successfully mounted in many other Canadian centres, including Toronto, Ottawa, Calgary, and Winnipeg, as well as in New York City. He's also created original works for student productions at Grant MacEwan University and the University of Alberta, and has frequently taught playwriting workshops for elementary classes for Edmonton Public Schools.

Lemoine is a six-time winner of Edmonton's Elizabeth Sterling Haynes Award for his work with Teatro, most recently for Outstanding New Fringe Play for *The Oculist's Holiday.* He has also won Toronto's Dora Mavor Moore Award for *The Vile Governess and Other Psychodramas.* His play *Pith!* won the New York International Fringe Festival's Award for Excellence in Playwriting following its appearance at the Festival in 2004, and was remounted there in August 2006 as part of the FringeNYC tenth anniversary celebrations. In May 2003, he was presented with the Queen's Golden Jubilee Medal by the Lieutenant Governor of Alberta, Lois Hole. In 2008, he was the first recipient of the Province of Alberta's Tommy Banks Award for Achievement in Performing Arts, and in 2010, he was inducted into the City of Edmonton's Cultural Hall of Fame.

¶ This book was typeset in Perpetua and Gill Sans designed by Eric Gill.